Style Guide

UNITED STATES CONFERENCE OF CATHOLIC BISHOPS

Liturgy Training Publications
3949 South Racine Avenue
Chicago, Illinois 60609
1-773-579-4900
www.LTP.org

United States Conference of Catholic Bishops
Washington, D.C.

First printing, March 2008

ISBN 978-1-60137-021-1

CONTENTS

Section A. Principles and Practices

Section B. Nuts and Bolts

Appendices

CHAPTER 1
How to Use This Guide

This *Style Guide* changes no current practices and establishes no new rules. Rather, it provides a single source describing practices in the existing house style for the United States Conference of Catholic Bishops (USCCB).

USCCB publications generally follow the *Chicago Manual of Style* (15th edition). In addition to presenting some *Chicago* guidelines in common use at the USCCB, this *Style Guide* also compiles deviations from *Chicago* and other style rules specific to USCCB needs.

Consistency of style is an essential element of effective publishing. This guide is intended for two audiences vital to publishing efforts at the United States Conference of Catholic Bishops:

1. The staff of the USCCB
2. Outside experts who write or edit material for the USCCB

This guide is divided into two sections (A and B):

A. **Principles and Practices.** This section provides helpful guiding principles specific to the nature and scope of USCCB publications.

IF YOU NEED TO	Cite the Bible, refer to major texts of the Catholic Church, or find official wording of traditional prayers	**SEE**	Chapter 2, "Preferred Editions: The Bible, the *Catechism*, and Other Sources"
IF YOU NEED TO	Quote from another source, cite a source, or learn about permission to use someone else's work	**SEE**	Chapter 3, "Other People's Words"

IF YOU NEED TO	Capitalize an important word, or use an abbreviation for a book of the Bible, state, etc.	**SEE**	Chapter 4, "Capitalization and Abbreviation"
IF YOU NEED TO	Refer to people in the Church, prayers, and Latin titles for church texts	**SEE**	Chapter 5, "Names and Titles of People and Things"
IF YOU NEED TO	Write about the Internet, use materials from the Internet, or publish to the USCCB Web site	**SEE**	Chapter 6, "The Internet"
IF YOU NEED TO	Determine the correct text for a prefatory statement, or add the USCCB copyright notice	**SEE**	Chapter 7, "Prefatory Statements, Decrees, and Copyright Notices"

B. Nuts and Bolts. This section includes chapters on more general topics relevant to USCCB publishing efforts.

IF YOU NEED TO	Write about race, gender or disabilities; review how to handle common word difficulties; or hyphenate or spell a word	**SEE**	Chapter 8, "Words"
IF YOU NEED TO	Find out how the USCCB handles common questions about grammar and punctuation	**SEE**	Chapter 9, "Grammar and Punctuation Notes"

IF YOU NEED TO	Find out whether to spell out a number, or how to format dates and phone numbers	SEE	Chapter 10, "Treatment of Numbers"
IF YOU NEED TO	Use italics, boldface, under-lining, all caps, or small caps	SEE	Chapter 11, "Italics, Boldface, and Others"

This guide also features two appendices:

1. **Appendix A.** This appendix provides guidelines for preparing manuscripts to go to USCCB Publishing.

2. **Appendix B.** This appendix provides approximate length counts for standard publication types and sizes.

Because style evolves with reader expectations and common practices, it is expected that this *USCCB Style Guide* will need to be updated periodically. Suggestions and additions may be sent to *styleguide@usccb.org*.

SECTION A
PRINCIPLES AND PRACTICES

CHAPTER 2
Preferred Editions: The Bible, the *Catechism*, and Other Sources

BIBLE

New American Bible

The official translation used by the USCCB is the *New American Bible* (NAB). More specifically, New Testament quotes must come from the 1986 NAB New Testament text; Old Testament quotes must come from the 1970 NAB Old Testament text; Psalms must come from either the 1970 or, for non-liturgical texts, the 1991 NAB Psalms. (The copyright page of the NAB edition that is used will tell the copyright dates of the texts included in that edition.)

If special circumstances dictate using another translation, then specifically identify the translation in the citation: NRSV, etc.

Lectionary

Use the *Lectionary for Mass* for all homily quotes, not the NAB.

Spanish Bible

The official source for Bible passages in Spanish is the *Leccionario Mexicano*, available in three volumes from Liturgical Press. A copy is available in USCCB Publishing. USCCB Publishing can also help locate passages not contained in the *Leccionario*.

CATECHISM OF THE CATHOLIC CHURCH

The USCCB edition is the preferred edition for English and Spanish. When citing, do not list an author.

> *Catechism of the Catholic Church* (2nd ed.). Washington, DC: Libreria Editrice Vaticana–United States Conference of Catholic Bishops, 2000.

> *Catecismo de la Iglesia Católica* (2a ed.). Washington, DC: Libreria Editrice Vaticana–United States Conference of Catholic Bishops, 2001.

SECOND VATICAN COUNCIL

Abbott translation

The 1966 translation by Walter M. Abbott, SJ, can be used without payment by the USCCB.

Abbott, Walter M., ed. *The Documents of Vatican II*. New York: Guild Press, 1966.

Flannery translation

The more recent translations by Austin Flannery, OP, are preferred for their up-to-date language. The USCCB does pay a fee depending on the amount quoted. Two main editions are available:

Flannery, Austin, ed. *Vatican Council II: Volume 1: The Conciliar and Post Conciliar Documents* (new rev. ed.). Northport, NY: Costello Publishing, 1996.

Flannery, Austin, ed. *The Basic Sixteen Documents: Vatican Council II: Constitutions, Decrees, Declarations*. Northport, NY: Costello Publishing, 1996.

Vatican Web site

Do not use the Vatican Web site for Second Vatican Council texts. Use either the Abbott or Flannery edition.

CANON LAW

For both the *Code of Canon Law* and the *Code of Canons of the Eastern Churches*, use the most recent translations by the Canon Law Society of America. When citing, do not list an author.

> *Code of Canon Law: Latin-English Edition: New English Translation* (*Codex Iuris Canonici* [CIC]). Washington, DC: Canon Law Society of America, 1998.
>
> *Code of Canons of the Eastern Churches: New English Translation* (*Codex Canonum Ecclesiarum Orientalium* [CCEO]). Washington, DC: Canon Law Society of America, 2001.

PAPAL AND HOLY SEE DOCUMENTS

USCCB editions　　Always use USCCB editions when they exist. USCCB Publishing has produced official editions of many papal and Vatican documents, containing the texts as approved by the Holy See. These titles include many papal letters and encyclicals, foundational texts such as the *Catechism* and the *General Directory for Catechesis*, and liturgical documents such as the *General Instruction of the Roman Missal*. Check the Publishing Web site (*www.usccbpublishing.com*) to see if a title is currently available; if it is not, Publishing may have an archived copy.

Vatican Web site　　Because the Vatican Web site (*www.vatican.va*) sometimes provides "provisional" texts, not final texts, only use the Vatican Web site when a text has not been published by USCCB Publishing. Cite the Vatican Web site accordingly.

CNS's Origins

Use USCCB editions and then Vatican Web site editions as first resorts in formal publications. Texts that are reprinted in *Origins* undergo a journalistic style edit that sometimes changes italics, capitalization, citations, and other elements. In general, use *Origins* texts only for texts that cannot be located in the first two categories of sources.

USCCB DOCUMENTS

Editions

If the USCCB has published an edition, cite the USCCB edition, even if it is out of print. (Other publishers have sometimes received licenses to reprint USCCB materials, but the USCCB cites its own editions wherever possible.)

Out-of-print texts

Publishing staff can sometimes locate a copy in Publishing's files.

TRADITIONAL PRAYERS

Official texts

Use the official texts of traditional prayers (Our Father, Hail Mary, etc.) as printed in the following sources:

United States Catholic Catechism for Adults. Washington, DC: United States Conference of Catholic Bishops, 2006.

Compendium of the Catechism of the Catholic Church. Washington, DC: United States Conference of Catholic Bishops, 2006.

Compendio del Catecismo de la Iglesia Católica. Washington, DC: United States Conference of Catholic Bishops, 2006.

Liturgical prayers   For prayers appearing in liturgical rites (including prayer services), official liturgical texts of standard prayers are to be used. The appropriate sources can be consulted in Publishing or the Secretariat of Divine Worship.

REFERENCES FOR WRITERS

Dictionaries   Two preferred editions are as follows. Subsequent editions are also acceptable.

Merriam-Webster's Collegiate Dictionary (11th ed.). Springfield, MA: Merriam-Webster, 2003.

The American Heritage College Dictionary (4th ed.). Boston: Houghton-Mifflin, 2002.

Writing/editing   Strunk and White's classic *The Elements of Style* is a must-read. Now in its fourth edition, it abounds in wisdom and good sense and is elegantly written.

Strunk, William, Jr. and E. B. White. *The Elements of Style* (4th ed.). New York: Longman, 2000.

Chicago Manual of Style   In addition to this *USCCB Style Guide*, use the *Chicago Manual of Style* for formal publications. "Chicago style" has also been rendered more user-friendly in the Turabian manuals.

The Chicago Manual of Style (15th ed.). Chicago: University of Chicago Press, 2003.

Turabian, Kate, ed. *A Manual for Writers of Term Papers, Theses, and Dissertations* (6th ed.). Chicago: University of Chicago Press, 1996.

Church style

Consult the *Catholic News Service Stylebook on Religion* for treatment of some abbreviations and Church references (such as degrees and orders). For all other non-journalistic publication questions, follow the *USCCB Style Guide*.

Catholic News Service. *CNS Style Book on Religion* (3rd ed.). Washington, DC: Catholic News Service, 2006.

Liturgical style

Consult the Secretariat for Divine Worship. Also, the 2007 *Ratio Translationis for the English Language*, from the Congregation for Divine Worship and the Discipline of the Sacraments, includes guidelines governing the production of liturgical materials.

Congregation for Divine Worship and the Discipline of the Sacraments. *Ratio Translationis for the English Language.* Washington, DC: United States Conference of Catholic Bishops, 2006.

Spanish style

A USCCB Spanish style guide is in development.

CHAPTER 3
Other People's Words

WHEN AND HOW TO CITE

When to cite

When in doubt, cite. Provide all information about the original publication (see "Three Elements Needed in Citation," later in this chapter) for the following cases:

- Quotations (of any length) and paraphrases
- Statistics
- Interviews
- Someone else's original idea
- Generalizations and other disputable assertions

First and subsequent citations

Provide the full citation, with all publication information, upon first reference. Subsequent references may truncate the source to the title or author's name, whichever is more important for the audience and purpose of the publication.

First: John Paul II, *Pastores Dabo Vobis* (*I Will Give You Shepherds*) (Washington, DC: United States Conference of Catholic Bishops, 1992).

Subsequent: *Pastores Dabo Vobis*, no. 60.

PDV, no. 60. *[if abbreviations are being used]*

Provide photocopies to Publishing

Upon giving a manuscript to Publishing, please provide photocopies for all quoted and cited material.

The photocopies should include the following for each source used:

- Title page
- Copyright page
- Pages of quoted/cited material (including statistics)

When quoting or citing from an Internet source, please provide printouts of the equivalent citation information, including the specific quoted material.

Elements of citations/references

As long as all the information is present and can be easily identified, Publishing can correct the style as needed. (See "Three Elements Needed in Citation," later in this chapter.)

QUOTATIONS

Quoting vs. Paraphrasing

Quotation

When a text repeats original material word for word, this is a quotation. Quotations must appear complete in the style in which they appear in the original source (except as indicated below, in "Altering Quoted Material").

Paraphrase

"Paraphrase" means summarizing another's idea in new words. It is not enough simply to change a word or two. True paraphrase bears little resemblance to the wording or sentence structure of the original passage. Most paraphrases, if summarizing a clearly identifiable passage in an original source, should be cited.

Quoting from the Bible and Ritual Texts: Special Needs

Sense lines

"Sense lines" are text formatted with line breaks (plus any indents), as in poetry or verse. The Bible contains many passages in sense lines (such as Isaiah, other Old Testament books, and several passages in the New Testament). Ritual texts (such as the *Lectionary for Mass*, *Rite of Confirmation*, etc.) also feature many passages in sense lines.

Because they are intentional, line breaks and indents are part of the quote and must be conveyed along with the words. See subsection below, "Formatting Different Kinds of Quotes," for more details about formatting sense lines.

Citation

See Chapter 4, "Capitalization and Abbreviation," for book abbreviations to use in Bible citations.

Changing quotes from the Bible, Vatican texts, and ritual texts

Do not change or eliminate italics, small caps (or all caps), punctuation, or capitalization in quotes from the Bible, ritual texts, or other Vatican documents. However, spelling and quotation marks (including punctuation with quotation marks) may be silently conformed to American rules, because they do not change content or meaning.

Altering Quoted Material

Identifying changes

Clearly identify any changes to the wording or intention of the quoted passage (except those noted below).

a. Place *additions* within brackets ([/]). If the writer has added emphasis, this should also be noted: "[emphasis added]."

b. Note *deletions* with ellipses (. . .). The standard ellipsis is three periods and four spaces (including one before and after the ellipsis). If the omission includes the end of a sentence, a four-period ellipsis is used, with no space between the last word and the first period.

Example: [original quote] "We also build this plan on the foundation of past strategies."

[altered quote] "We . . . build this plan [for young adult ministry] on the foundation of past strategies."

[altered quote] "We recognize a certain urgency in developing this plan as a result of the listening sessions. . . . [which] provided us with valuable insights."

Changes not needing identification

The following changes can be made to quoted material without needing to identify the changes:

a. The first letter of a quotation may be changed to capital or lowercase, as needed. Do not use brackets to denote this change.
b. Do not use ellipses at the beginning or end of quotations.
c. The final punctuation mark may be changed, and punctuation may be left out where ellipses are used.
d. In a quotation from a modern source, an indisputable typographic error may be corrected without identifying the change. ("*Sic*," meaning "thus," is rarely used.)

Special cases

a. Original footnote or endnote references in quoted material may sometimes be abbreviated. Always retain any Bible citations in quoted material.

If the decision is made to include any original citations in quotes that are used in a new document that is also using note citations, integrate them into the citations of the new document and renumber accordingly. As always, consider the intended purpose and audience of the new document.

b. When an entire statement or article is being reprinted, capitalization, punctuation, and spelling may be conformed to USCCB style, provided that they are not used specially for effect in the original source.

Formatting Different Kinds of Quotes

General rule

Quoted material that exceeds eight typed lines is set off from the text, or "blocked," without quotation marks. Shorter quotations should be integrated into (or "run into") the text itself, with double quotation marks.

Run-In (or In-Text) Quotes

Introducing quotes

If a quotation is grammatically seamless with the sentence, no introductory punctuation is needed, and the first word of the quote is not capitalized. If the quotation is introduced (e.g., "The bishops said"), then the quotation is preceded by a comma or colon, and the first word of the quote is capitalized.

Incorrect: The bishops said that, "We . . . build this plan on the foundation of past strategies." *["That" makes the quote a grammatical part of the sentence.]*

Correct: The bishops said, "We . . . build this plan on the foundation of past strategies."

| *Correct:* | The bishops said that they "build this plan on the foundation of past strategies." |

End punctuation

The quotation mark goes outside the period, comma, exclamation point, or question mark; it precedes any semicolon or colon. (See Chapter 9, "Grammar and Punctuation Notes," for more detailed discussion of quotation marks and punctuation.)

| *Example:* | The bishops said that they "build this plan on the foundation of past strategies." |

| *Example:* | The bishops said that they "build this plan on the foundation of past strategies"; they undertook extensive consultation before drafting *Sons and Daughters of the Light*. |

Citation placement

Cite a run-in quote with either a parenthetical citation, a footnote, or an endnote. Insert a parenthetical citation between the quotation mark and the ending punctuation. If using notes instead, the note number follows the quotation mark (or the semicolon or colon, if applicable).

| *Example:* | The bishops stated, "We . . . build this plan on the foundation of past strategies" (*Sons and Daughters of the Light*, 25). |

| *Example:* | The bishops stated, "We . . . build this plan on the foundation of past strategies."[1]
[1] *Sons and Daughters of the Light*, 25. |

Block Quotes

Block format

Indent block quotes one half-inch on the left margin; they are typically preceded and followed by a line space. Omit the quotation marks. Do not reduce the type size or add other styles (such as italics not found in the original).

Citation placement

Parenthetical citations and note numbers both follow the final punctuation of a block quote.

Example: Jesus first preached in the synagogue by reading a prophetic passage from Isaiah:

> The Spirit of the Lord is upon me,
> because he has anointed me
> to bring glad tidings to
> the poor. (Lk 4:18)

Example: Jesus first preached in the synagogue by reading a prophetic passage from Isaiah:

> The Spirit of the Lord is upon me,
> because he has anointed me
> to bring glad tidings to
> the poor.[1]

[1] Lk 4:18.

Sense Lines (Verse)

Definition

"Sense lines" are text formatted with line breaks (plus indents, sometimes), as in poetry or verse. Because they are intentional, line breaks and indents are part of the quote and must be conveyed along with the words. (See previous discussion in this chapter on "Quoting from the Bible," since the Bible has numerous passages in sense lines.)

Formatting

When quoting from text formatted in sense lines, choose from two options for preserving the sense lines:

a. Copy the format exactly. Format like a block quote, and break and indent the lines exactly as shown in the original source. (As with a block quote, this situation would not use quotation marks, and the citation would follow the end punctuation.)

Example: Jesus first preached in the synagogue by reading a prophetic passage from Isaiah:

> The Spirit of the Lord is upon me,
> because he has anointed me
> to bring glad tidings to
> the poor. (Lk 4:18)

b.   Use slashes (/), flanked by a space on either side, to show line breaks. Choose this option if you want to "run in" the quote with the paragraph, rather than set it off as a block quote. (Note that the citation precedes the end punctuation.)

Example: Jesus first preached in the synagogue by reading a prophetic passage from Isaiah: "The Spirit of the Lord is upon me, / because he has anointed me / to bring glad tidings to the poor" (Lk 4:18).

Epigraphs

Definition   An epigraph is a quotation used to introduce a book, chapter, or section.

Citing   Provide full citations for epigraphs that introduce chapters or sections. (Epigraphs that introduce books are typically provided with minimal attribution: the source's name and perhaps a date.)

DOCUMENTATION AND CITATION

Identifying Exact Location of Source

Paragraph numbers   Cite by paragraph number whenever possible. Many church documents have numbered paragraphs. This convention allows one to look up a given passage in any edition.

Use "no." or "nos." to cite one or more paragraph numbers. Do not use the paragraph symbol (¶) or "n./nn."

Example: [1] *Presbyterorum ordinis*, nos. 4-6; see *Pastores Dabo Vobis*, no. 26.

Page numbers

If the source's paragraphs are not numbered, cite by the page number. Do not use "page" or "p./pp."—simply give the number. (Do not cite by chapter or section numbers, which are too general for precise citation.)

Bible citations

Use a colon to separate chapter and verse, with no space on either side. Use a comma to separate non-consecutive verses. For ranges of verses, use a hyphen if the range is contained within a chapter; use an en-dash to cite a passage that spans more than one chapter. (See Chapter 9, "Grammar and Punctuation Notes," for more information about dashes.)

In the body of a text, spell out the full book of the Bible. In citations (parenthetical or notes), use the Bible book abbreviations provided in Chapter 4, "Capitalization and Abbreviation."

Example: [1] See Mt 27:62–28:10. See also Mk 16:1-8.

Example: In Matthew 6:9-13, Jesus taught us how to pray.

Canon citations

In citations of canon law, use "c." or "cc." to cite one or more canons, respectively. (Note that "canon" should otherwise be spelled out in the body of a text.)

Example: [1] See *Code of Canon Law* (CIC), cc. 254, 256; *Code of Canons of the Eastern Churches* (CCEO), c. 352.

Cite precisely, including the "§" for a section or "°" for subsection of the exact canon cited. Take care to apply these symbols accurately. For multiple sections, double the "§" symbol; for multiple subsections ("°") simply repeat the symbol. See the examples below, especially for spacing and punctuation guidance.

Example: [1] See *Code of Canon Law* (CIC), cc. 253 §1, 254 §§1-2.
            [2] CIC, c. 190 1°-2°.
            [3] CIC, cc. 1091 §§1, 3; 1095 1°, 3°.

Footnotes, Endnotes, and Parenthetical Citation

Consistency

In general, use just one form of citation in a document: footnotes, endnotes, or parenthetical citations. (On rare occasions, a special need may dictate using two forms: e.g., parenthetical citations for bibliographic information, plus footnotes for substantive notes.)

Footnotes, endnotes

Whichever type of note is used, identify a note with a superscripted number in the text, corresponding to a numbered note elsewhere— footnotes at the "foot" of the page, and endnotes at the end of the text (e.g., at the end of the document or at the end of each chapter).

The first note for each source should provide the full source information, as well as the page or paragraph number(s) of the material cited by that particular note. Because the information is self-contained, the publication needs no bibliography (though a resource list may still be useful).

Example: Those who encourage forgiveness to resolve international conflict have been described as "voices in the geopolitical wilderness."[1]

            [1] William Bole, Drew Christiansen, SJ, and Robert T. Hennemeyer, *Forgiveness in International Politics: An Alternative Road to Peace* (Washington, DC: United States Conference of Catholic Bishops, 2004), 27.

In-text citations (parenthetical)

These give a brief reference within the text itself, in parentheses, rather than in a note. The source is identified by author or truncated title. Provide the source's full information in a bibliography or resource list at the end of the text.

> *Example:* Those who encourage forgiveness to resolve international conflict have been described as "voices in the geopolitical wilderness" (*Forgiveness*, 27).
>
> [Bibliography Entry]
> Bole, William, Drew Christiansen, SJ, and Robert T. Hennemeyer. *Forgiveness in International Politics: An Alternative Road to Peace.* Washington, DC: United States Conference of Catholic Bishops, 2004.

Three Elements Needed in Citation

Follow the *Chicago Manual of Style* guidelines for documentation of sources, except where this *Style Guide* specifically departs from those guidelines. This section provides information about the most commonly used sources, but authors and editors should consult the *Chicago Manual* for special cases.

Three elements

In general, documentation of sources must specify the following three elements: *authorship*, *title*, and *publication information*.

a. Author(s), including (as applicable)
   - Corporate author (e.g., the USCCB, or the Center for Applied Research in the Apostolate [CARA])
   - Artists
   - Interview sources as "authors"
   - Editors or translators, if more germane to the source

    b. Title of source, according to the type of source used
- Book (including proceedings, standalone studies, etc.)
- Chapter or essay in a book (if applicable); give title of book as well
- Article and periodical
- Web page (including URL and name of Web page)
- Movie, video, or album
- Personal communication or interview
- Work of art

    c. Publication information
- For books: city, publisher, and year
- For periodicals: date, volume and issue number, page numbers of article
- For online sources: URL (Web address)
- For works of art: present location

Consider specifying the genre of Vatican sources in their citations ("encyclical letter," "apostolic exhortation," etc.), when appropriate for the intended audience and purpose.

Books, Booklets, and Brochures

In footnote/endnote

The footnote or endnote format for citing a book is as follows.

Author, *Book Title* (City, State: Publisher, Year), Page.

In notes, provide authors' names (if individuals) first-name first. Be sure to provide the page or paragraph number of the material cited, unless the note is a general suggestion to "see" a source.

Examples: [1] USCCB Administrative Committee, *Faithful Citizenship: A Catholic Call to Political Responsibility* (Washington, DC: United States Conference of Catholic Bishops, 2003), 12.

[2] William Bole, Drew Christiansen, SJ, and Robert T. Hennemeyer, *Forgiveness in International Politics: An Alternative Road to Peace* (Washington, DC: United States Conference of Catholic Bishops, 2004), 27.

[3] See Second Vatican Council, *Vatican Council II: Volume 1: The Conciliar and Post Conciliar Documents*, ed. Austin Flannery (Northport, NY: Costello Publishing, 1996).

In bibliography

When the source appears in a reference list, resource list, or bibliography, it is formatted in a slightly different order. In general, organize the list alphabetically using the first word of each entry.

Author. *Book Title*. City, State: Publisher, Year.

In bibliographies, give the first (or only) author's name in the order of last-name first, if the author is an individual. (Note that subsequent authors for that source are provided first-name first.)

Examples: Bole, William, Drew Christiansen, SJ, and Robert T. Hennemeyer. *Forgiveness in International Politics: An Alternative Road to Peace*. Washington, DC: United States Conference of Catholic Bishops, 2004.

Second Vatican Council. *Vatican Council II: Volume 1: The Conciliar and Post Conciliar Documents*. Edited by Austin Flannery. Northport, NY: Costello Publishing, 1996.

> USCCB Administrative Committee. *Faithful Citizenship: A Catholic Call to Political Responsibility.* Washington, DC: United States Conference of Catholic Bishops, 2003.

Titled Parts of Books (Chapters, Essays)

In footnote/endnote

The footnote or endnote format for citing an essay or chapter is as follows:

Author, "Chapter or Essay Title," in *Book Title* (City, State: Publisher, Year), Page.

In notes, give the authors' names (if individuals) first-name first. Be sure to provide the page or paragraph number of the material cited. If the note is a general suggestion to "see" a source, provide the full page range.

Examples:

1   Cardinal Roger M. Mahony, "Preaching the Gospel in the New Millennium: Obstacles and Hopes," in *Priests for a New Millennium: A Series of Essays on the Ministerial Priesthood by the Catholic Bishops of the United States* (Washington, DC: United States Conference of Catholic Bishops, 2000), 93.

2   Second Vatican Council, *Constitution on the Sacred Liturgy (Sacrosanctum Concilium)*, no. 12, in *Vatican Council II: Volume 1: The Conciliar and Post Conciliar Documents*, ed. Austin Flannery (Northport, NY: Costello Publishing, 1996).

In the example of *Sacrosanctum Concilium*, because it is a stand-alone piece anthologized in a collection, the title is put in italics, not in quotation marks.

In bibliography

When the source appears in a reference list, resource list, or bibliography, it is formatted in a slightly different order.

In general, organize the list alphabetically using the first word of each entry.

Author. "Chapter or Essay Title." In *Book Title*, Pages. City, State: Publisher, Year.

In bibliographies, give the first (or only) author's name in the order of last-name first, if the author is an individual. (Subsequent authors for the source are provided first-name first.) Also be sure to cite the full page range for the chapter or essay.

Examples: Mahony, Cardinal Roger M. "Preaching the Gospel in the New Millennium: Obstacles and Hopes." In *Priests for a New Millennium: A Series of Essays on the Ministerial Priesthood by the Catholic Bishops of the United States*, 91-111. Washington, DC: United States Conference of Catholic Bishops, 2000.

Second Vatican Council. *Constitution on the Sacred Liturgy (Sacrosanctum Concilium)*. In *Vatican Council II: Volume 1: The Conciliar and Post-Conciliar Documents*, edited by Austin Flannery. Northport, NY: Costello Publishing, 1996.

In the example of *Sacrosanctum Concilium*, because it is a stand-alone piece anthologized in a collection, the title is put in italics, not in quotation marks.

Articles in Periodicals

In footnote/endnote   The footnote or endnote format for citing an article in a periodical is as follows:

Author, "Article Title," *Periodical Title* Volume Number: Issue Number (Date): Pages.

In notes, give the authors' names (if individuals) first-name first. Be sure to provide the page(s) of the material cited. If the note is a general suggestion to "see" a source, provide the full page range.

Examples: [1] See Stephen Wilbricht, "The Religious and Cultural Meaning of the Mexican American *Quinceañera," The Living Light* 40:3 (Spring 2004): 70-81.

           [2] Doris Murphy, "How to Teach with Christmas Carols," *RTJ: The Magazine for Catechist Formation* 40:7 (November/December 2004): 11.

In bibliography

When the source appears in a reference list, resource list, or bibliography, it is formatted in a slightly different order. In general, organize the list alphabetically using the first word of each entry.

Author. "Article Title." *Periodical Title* **Volume Number: Issue Number (Date): Pages.**

In bibliographies, give the first (or only) author's name in the order of last-name first, if the author is an individual. (Subsequent authors for the source are provided first-name first.) Be sure to cite the full page range for the article.

Examples: Murphy, Doris. "How to Teach with Christmas Carols." *RTJ: The Magazine for Catechist Formation* 40:7 (November/December 2004): 11-12.

          Wilbricht, Stephen. "The Religious and Cultural Meaning of the Mexican American *Quinceañera." The Living Light* 40:3 (Spring 2004): 70-81.

Special Cases

Interviews, personal communications

Cite original interviews conducted for the project, as well as personal communications (letters, e-mails, and so on). They are only cited in text—via note or parenthetical citation—not in a bibliography.

Typically, the source of the interview or letter is the "author." Because these sources do not have titles, describe them without quotation marks or italics. Do not provide individuals' e-mail addresses without their permission.

Notes:

[1] William Vendley, telephone interview with William Bole, July 2001.

[2] Catherine Rothwell, e-mail message to author, January 29, 2004.

[3] Jane Smith, post to DCPubs Yahoo! group, October 21, 2004, *groups.yahoo.com/group/dcpubs/message/19985.*

Online Sources

In footnote/endnote

The footnote or endnote format for citing an online source is as follows:

Author, "Web Page Title," *Web Site Name*, URL (accessed Date).

The date of access should be cited when a given Internet site is subject to change. The date fixes the source at a specific moment in time.

Examples:

[1] USCCB Office of Child and Youth Protection, "Who We Are," *United States Conference of Catholic Bishops, www.usccb.org/ocyp/whoweare.htm* (accessed December 16, 2004).

[2] David McGuire, "Uncertain Landscape Ahead for Copyright Protection," *Washington Post*, December 16, 2004, *www.washingtonpost.com/wp-dyn/articles/A4003-2004Dec16.html* (accessed December 17, 2004).

In bibliography

When the source appears in a reference list, resource list, or bibliography, it is formatted in a slightly different manner. In general, organize the list alphabetically using the first word of each entry.

Author. "Web Page Title." *Web Site Name.* URL (accessed Date).

The date of access should be cited when a given Internet site is subject to change. The date fixes the source at a specific moment in time.

Examples:

McGuire, David. "Uncertain Landscape Ahead for Copyright Protection." *Washington Post*, December 16, 2004. *www.washingtonpost.com/wp-dyn/articles/A4003-2004Dec16.html* (accessed December 17, 2004).

USCCB Office of Child and Youth Protection. "Who We Are." *United States Conference of Catholic Bishops. www.usccb.org/ocyp/whoweare.htm* (accessed December 16, 2004).

Common Abbreviations and Notations

The following notations are commonly used in citations and references. Note that some are rarely used and are not recommended.

NOTATION	MEANING
Cf.	"Confer," "compare," "contrast with." Does not mean "see."
See	"For more information, consult." Distinct from "cf."
Ibid.	"See source just cited." Usually only used in notes, not in parenthetical citations. Not recommended, since it can easily get separated from the source to which it refers during drafting and editing.
Idem	"The same," usually referring to author. Do not use; rather, repeat the author's last name and/or a truncated title for each citation.
f./ff.	"And following." Often used when citing Bible verses or lines of poetry. Do include the ending period.
loc. cit. and op. cit.	"In the place cited" and "in the work cited," respectively. Do not use; rather, repeat the author's last name and/or a truncated title for each citation.

COPYRIGHT AND PERMISSION

USCCB copyright   The copyright on materials produced by the Conference is held by the United States Conference of Catholic Bishops. It is not held by the committee, office, secretariat, department, or individual that produced the text. The group or person listed as the author of a work is not necessarily the copyright holder.

If the author or editor of a work is not a member of the Conference staff or a bishop, a contract is necessary before work begins. Consult with the Office of General

Counsel to obtain contracts. See below for discussion of different types of contracts possible.

When Must Permission Be Sought?

Permissions review

When in doubt, committees and their staffs should consult the Office of General Counsel. All material published through USCCB Publishing is reviewed by the Associate Director for Copyrights and Permissions, who determines what quoted/reprinted material requires licenses and permission requests.

Common myths

The following *misconceptions* are explained further in this section:

- "Copyright laws don't apply to non-profits like the USCCB."
- "If we aren't going to sell it, we don't need permission."
- "No permission is needed for Church documents such as the Vatican II documents, liturgical texts, and the Bible."
- "We don't need permission for Vatican texts."
- "If there's no copyright notice on something, it's in the public domain."
- "We paid the author [photographer, artist, etc.] for the work, so we own the copyright."
- "If it's more than fifty [seventy-five, etc.] years old, it's in the public domain."
- "If it's fewer than 500 [300, 250, etc.] words, it's fair use."

Ownership and Date of Copyright

Ownership

As a rule, the actual creator of the work owns the copyright, unless agreed otherwise in writing prior to the beginning of work. The exception is when employees do work within the scope of their employment, in which case the employer owns the copyright.

Definition and start of copyright

The copyright begins from the moment that a work is created in a fixed form (e.g., print, computer file, photograph, etc.). For works for hire created after January 1, 1978, copyright generally lasts for 95 years.

Differences Between Work for Hire, Assignment of Rights, Licenses, and Releases

Work for hire

A *work-for-hire contract* must be signed before work begins. Under our standard work-for-hire agreement, the USCCB owns the copyright and can use the product in any way it chooses. The creator retains no rights in the copyrighted work.

Section 101 of the copyright law defines a work for hire as:

1. a work prepared by an employee within the scope of his or her employment; or
2. a work specially ordered or commissioned for use as a contribution to a collective work, as a part of a motion picture or other audiovisual work, as a translation, as a supplementary work, as a compilation, as an instructional text, as a test, as answer material for a test, or as an atlas, if the parties expressly agree in a written instrument signed by them that the work shall be considered a work made for hire. For the purpose of the foregoing

sentence, a "supplementary work" is a work prepared for publication as a secondary adjunct to a work by another author for the purpose of introducing, concluding, illustrating, explaining, revising, commenting upon, or assisting in the use of the other work, such as forewords, afterwords, pictorial illustrations, maps, charts, tables, editorial notes, musical arrangements, answer material for tests, bibliographies, appendixes, and indexes, and an "instructional text" is a literary, pictorial, or graphic work prepared for publication and with the purpose of use in systematic instructional activities.

Assignment of rights

An *assignment of rights* is signed after work has begun, though the work may or may not be complete. If the rights are assigned to the USCCB, the USCCB owns the copyright and can use the product in any way it chooses. The creator retains no rights in the copyrighted work.

Licenses

A *license* allows the USCCB to use a copyrighted work in specified ways for a specified period of time or number of copies. Any additional uses must be negotiated separately. The creator retains the copyright. When negotiating license agreements, please consult the Office of General Counsel for guidance.

Releases

Releases are necessary in a variety of circumstances common to USCCB work, including use of photos featuring individuals, video footage from diocesan or Conference events, and quotes by individuals. Releases are necessary to ensure the privacy of the individuals involved. Consult with the Office of General Counsel to obtain release forms that people can sign or to obtain notices that may be posted at taped events.

USCCB Policies

Rights typically used by the USCCB

Print, electronic, digital, promotional, sublicensing, and derivative works (especially translations and abridgements) are the rights typically used by the USCCB. The USCCB also enforces copyright on everything it produces. Note that copyrighting a text does not prevent its widespread use.

General Counsel

The Office of General Counsel has issued "Copyright Procedures" that outline these principles in greater detail for the USCCB. A copy can be found on the staff-only Web site, *staff.usccb.org*, under "Publishing."

How to get permission

You can take several steps to facilitate the process for ensuring that the USCCB has the necessary permission to use someone else's words:

- Keep copies of all contracts and releases regarding the document.
- Quote, where possible, from texts listed in Chapter 2, "Preferred Editions."
- For any other text quoted, photocopy the title page, copyright page, and the page quoted for submission to USCCB Publishing.

CHAPTER 4
Capitalization and Abbreviation

CAPITALIZATION GENERAL RULES

Proper nouns

Capitalize the unique or official titles of organizations and groups. Unless provided as a legal or official name, the common noun should be the default and should be lowercased.

Example: The St. Benedict Parish Council authored the cookbook.

Example: The parish council adjourned.

Not used
for emphasis

Lowercase the names of positions, areas of study, schools of thought, and other such labels. They are common nouns, not proper nouns. Do not use capitalization merely to indicate emphasis or importance.

Example: Then-Msgr. Dennis Schnurr was general secretary of the Conference in 1999.

Example: Parish priests with questions about the new norms should consult the bishop.

Example: She received her master's degrees in philosophy and foreign policy.

Hyphenated words
in titles

When a hyphenated word is to be capitalized, capitalize all parts of the hyphenated word. (This excludes, as usual, prepositions and articles.)

Example: One-Eyed Man Kidnaps Trojan War Hero

Example: Up-to-Date Web Sites Hard to Maintain

"The" at beginning of names/titles	Do not capitalize "the" at the beginning of names and titles when used in a sentence. (One exception is The Catholic Relief Services Collection.)

Example:	The George Washington University [*official name*]
Example:	She graduated from the George Washington University.

Words in titles	Do not capitalize articles or most prepositions in titles. Do capitalize prepositions of five letters or longer (e.g., "between," "about").

Truncated names	USCCB names that are truncated after first reference retain the capitalization of the full reference.

Example:	United States Conference of Catholic Bishops; the Conference
Example:	Catholic Home Missions Appeal; the Appeal

In lists	In bulleted or numbered lists, capitalize the first word (even if the item is not a complete sentence).

USCCB CAPITALIZATION GUIDE[1]

General Principles for Religious Words

See next section for specific capitalization tables by categories.

Titles	• Titles of God and persons of the Trinity are always capitalized.
	• References to Jesus/God are capitalized, especially if the reference is a generic one and readers may

---

1   This capitalization guide has been reviewed by the Secretariat of Evangelization and Catechesis, the Secretariat of Doctrine, and the Secretariat of Divine Worship.

not recognize it (e.g., "the Word" when referring to Jesus, or even the "Other" in philosophical use when referring specifically to God).

- Pronouns referring to God ("he," "him") are lowercased.
- Titles given to Jesus and Mary are always capitalized.

  Redeemer, Savior, Mary Mother of God, Queen of Peace

- Titles of prayers are capitalized.

  Memorare, **Our Father, Hail Mary**

- Parts of the Mass are capitalized.

  Liturgy of the Word, *Gloria*, **Doxology**

- Nouns relating to the Bible are capitalized. When used as adjectives, they are lowercased.

  Scripture, Gospels, Gospel, scriptural scholarship, gospel values

Sacraments and mysteries

- Mysteries in the lives of Jesus and Mary are capitalized. Some titles are official names (without other meanings) and are capitalized (e.g., Pentecost, the Last Supper). Whenever the event is used in the context of a liturgical celebration, it should be capitalized as well (e.g., the Solemnity of the Annunciation, the Solemnity of the Ascension).
- Names of sacraments, such as Baptism or Anointing of the Sick, are capitalized as nouns. When used as verbs or adjectives, they are lowercased.
- The names of sacramentals, such as "rosary" or "scapular," are lowercased. "Rosary" is capitalized when it refers to the prayer and not the object.
- Unless used in the title of a specific blessing, "blessing" is lowercased.

- The word "rite" is not capitalized in reference to a sacrament unless the word is part of the title.

The Church

- References to the Church are capitalized, including "People of God" or "Body of Christ."
- The word "Church" itself is capitalized as a noun when referring to the Roman, Catholic, and Universal Church.
- "Church" as an adjective is lowercased: "church teaching," "church leaders."
- "Church" is also lowercased when referring in general, not specifically, to church(es).
- Ecumenical references and dialogues in particular lowercase church when referring in the generic, not the specific.
- Both "she" and "her" are acceptable when referring to the Catholic Church.
- The word "rite" should not be used when referring to Eastern Churches; the correct designation is "Church." E.g., "Byzantine Rite" needs to be replaced with "Byzantine Church." (See USCCB, *Eastern Catholics in the United States of America*, 1999.)

Tradition

- The term "Tradition" is capitalized when referring to the specifically inspired and formal establishment of church teaching and practice, oral and written.
- The Deposit of Faith is handed on in both Sacred Scripture and Sacred Tradition.
- The term "tradition" is lowercased when referring to general practices not apostolic nor inspired.

Capitalization Listing, by Uppercase/Lowercase

Uppercased

Act of Contrition
Advent
Advocate (title of Mary)
Amen (when used at conclusion
   of prayer)
Angelus (the)
Annunciation
Anointed One
Anointing of the Sick
Apostles, the
Apostles, Twelve
Archdiocese/Diocese (only when
   part of formal name)
Ascension
Ash Wednesday
Assumption
Baptism
Beatific Vision
Beatitudes
Benediction
Benefactress (as title of Mary)
Bible
Bishop of Rome
Blessed Mother
Blessed Sacrament
Blessed Virgin Mary
Blood of Christ
Body of Christ
Capital Sins
Cardinal(s) (only when used with
   proper names)
Cardinal Virtues
Chosen People
Christ
Christian(s)

Christmas
Church (as noun)
Closing Prayer (as part of Mass)
College of Bishops
Commandment (one of the Ten or
   Two Great)
Communion (Holy)
Communion of Saints
Confirmation
Consecration
Council (Second Vatican only)
Council Fathers (Second
   Vatican only)
Creator
Creed (Nicene, Apostles')
Crucifixion (of Christ)
Death (of Christ)
Decalogue
Deposit of Faith
Devil
Divine Inspiration
Divine Office
Divine Revelation
Divine Truth
Doctors (of the Church)
Doxology
Easter (Sunday)
Ecumenical Council
Elevation (at Mass)
Emmanuel
Epiphany
Epistles
Eternal Word
Eucharist (Holy)
Eucharistic Prayer   *(continued)*

Uppercased (continued)

Evangelist(s) (the four)
Ever Virgin (title of Mary)
Father (as title)
Fathers (of the Church or Council)
Feast (referring to proper name)
Glory Be (prayer)
God the Father
God the Holy Spirit
God the Son
Good Friday
Good News
Good Shepherd
Gospel
Hail, Holy Queen
Hail Mary
Handmaid of the Lord
Head of the Church
High Priest
Holy City (of Jerusalem)
Holy Family (Jesus, Mary,
   and Joseph)
Holy Matrimony
Holy One
Holy One of God
Holy Orders
Holy See
Holy Spirit
Holy Thursday
Holy Trinity
Holy Week
I AM
Immaculate Mary
Incarnation
Inspiration
Jesus
Jesus of Nazareth

Jesus the Galilean
Jesus Christ
Jewish People
Judgment Day
King (as title)
King Eternal
King of Glory
King of Israel
King of the Jews
Kingdom of God
Kingdom of Heaven
Kyrios (Lord)
Lamb of God
Last Day
Last Judgment
Last Supper
Latin Rite
Law (Old Testament Law)
Lectionary (as title)
Lent
Liturgy of the Eucharist
Liturgy of the Hours
Liturgy of the Word
Lord
Lord of Hosts
Lord's Day
Magisterium
Magnificat
Mass
Master (as title of Christ)
Matrimony (Sacrament of)
Memorare
Memorial (referring to proper name)
Messiah
Mother (as title of Mary)
Mother of God   *(continued)*

Uppercased *(continued)*

Mystical Body of Christ
New Adam
New Eve
New Testament
Old Testament
Only-Begotten Son
Opening Prayer (as part of Mass)
Original Sin
Our Father
Our Lady of (Lourdes, etc.)
Palm Sunday
Paraclete
Paschal (Mystery, Sacrifice)
Passion (in reference to Christ's)
Penitential Rite
Pentateuch
Pentecost
People of God
Persons (as regards the Three
   Persons of the Trinity)
Pope (specific designation, e.g.,
   Pope Benedict XVI)
Precious Body and Blood
Prince of Peace
Prophets, the Law and the
Purgatory
Queen of Heaven and Earth
Queen of Peace
Redeemer
Reign of God
Responsorial Psalm
Resurrection (of Christ)
Revelation
Roman Pontiff
Rosary (the prayer)
Sabbath (as day of the week)

Sacrament of Penance
   and Reconciliation
Sacramentary
Satan
Savior
Scripture(s) (Holy, Sacred)
Seat of Wisdom
Second Vatican Council
Servant (as title)
Seven Sacraments (the)
Shepherd
Solemnity (referring to proper name)
Son (as title)
Son of David
Son of the Father
Son of God
Son of Israel
Son of Man
Son of the Most High
Spirit (as Third Person of the Trinity)
Suffering Servant
Teacher
Temple, Jerusalem
Ten Commandments
Theotokos
Three-in-One
Tradition (Sacred)
Transfiguration
Trinitarian
Trinity
Trinity, Holy
Twelve, the
Virgin Mary
Word (referring to Jesus)
Word of God (referring to Bible)
Word of the Lord

Lowercased

angels
apostles (apart from the Twelve)
apostolic
biblical
bishop(s) (when not used with or in
   place of name)
brother(s)
canon of Scripture
canon law (unless part of title of
   book)
cardinal(s) (when not used with or in
   place of name)
Catholic / social / teaching
church (adj. or as building)
commandment (unless part of
   proper name)
conciliar (adj.)
confession
cross (not Christ's)
deacon(s) (when not used with or in
   place of name)
demons
episcopate, episcopacy
father(s) (when not used with or in
   place of name)
gospel (adj.)
heaven

hell
hierarchy
holy water
marriage
mystery
original justice
pope (when not used with or in
   place of name)
precepts of the Church
priest(s)
prophet (generic)
psalm(s) (if not the Book of Psalms)
redemption
resurrection (of the dead)
rite (when not used with the name)
rosary (the object)
sabbath (as modifier)
sacrament(s) (when not used with
   the name)
sacramental(s)
sacrifice of Christ
scriptural
second coming
sister(s)
social teaching (Catholic)
synoptic
tabernacle

Capitalization Listing, by Categories

Titles of God/Trinity

Christ	Paraclete
Creator	Persons (as regards the Three
Father	Persons of the Trinity)
God the Father	Son
God the Son	Son of God
God the Holy Spirit	Spirit (as Third Person of the Trinity)
Holy Spirit	Three-in-One
Holy Trinity	Trinitarian
Jesus	Trinity

Titles Given to Jesus

Anointed One	Lord of Hosts
Christ	Master
Emmanuel	Messiah
Eternal Word	New Adam
Good Shepherd	Only-Begotten Son
Head of the Church	Priest
High Priest	Prince of Peace
Holy One	Redeemer
Holy One of God	Savior
I AM	Servant
Jesus Christ	Shepherd
Jesus the Galilean	Son of David
Jesus of Nazareth	Son of Israel
King (as title)	Son (as title)
King Eternal	Son of the Father
King of Glory	Son of God
King of Israel	Son of Man
King of the Jews	Son of the Most High
Kyrios (Lord)	Suffering Servant
Lamb of God	Teacher
Lord	Word

Titles Given to Mary

Advocate
Benefactress
Blessed Mother
Blessed Virgin Mary
Ever Virgin
Handmaid of the Lord
Holy Family (Jesus, Mary, and
  Joseph)
Immaculate Mary

Mother of God
Mother
New Eve
Our Lady of (Lourdes, etc.)
Queen of Heaven and Earth
Queen of Peace
Seat of Wisdom
Theotokos
Virgin Mary

Liturgical/Sacramental Terms

Advent
Annunciation
Anointing of the Sick
Ascension
Ash Wednesday
Assumption
Baptism
Blessed Sacrament
Body of Christ
Christmas
Confirmation
Communion (Holy)
Easter (Sunday)
Emmanuel
Epiphany
Eucharist (Holy)
Feast (referring to proper noun)
Good Friday
Good News
Gospel

Holy Orders
Holy Matrimony
Holy Thursday
Holy Week
Holy Saturday
Lectionary (as title)
Lent
Lord's Day
Mass
Matrimony (Sacrament of)
Memorial (referring to proper noun)
Palm Sunday
Pentecost
Sacrament of Penance
  and Reconciliation
Sacramentary
Seven Sacraments (the)
Solemnity (referring to
  proper noun)
Transfiguration

The Mass: Its Parts and Associated Terms

Amen (at conclusion of prayer)	Lectionary
Benediction	Liturgy of the Word
Blessed Sacrament	Liturgy of the Eucharist
Blood of Christ	Lord
Body of Christ	Lord's Day
Closing Prayer	Mass
Communion (Holy)	Opening Prayer
Consecration	Penitential Rite
Creed (Nicene, Apostles')	Precious Body and Blood
Doxology	Responsorial Psalm
Elevation	Sacramentary
Epistles	Scripture(s) (Holy, Sacred)
Eucharist (Holy)	Word (referring to Jesus)
Gospel (noun)	Word of God (referring to Bible)
Last Supper	Word of the Lord
Latin Rite	

Titles of Prayers

Angelus (the)	Hail Mary
Act of Contrition	Hail, Holy Queen
Creed (Nicene, Apostles')	Liturgy of the Hours
Divine Office	*Magnificat*
Doxology	*Memorare*
Eucharistic Prayer	Our Father
Glory Be	Rosary (the prayer)

Theological, Church, and Scriptural Terms

Apostles, the	Beatitudes	
Apostles, Twelve	Bible	
Archdiocese/Diocese (only when part of formal name)	Bishop of Rome	
	Blood of Christ	
Beatific Vision	Body of Christ	*(continued)*

Theological, Church, and Scriptural Terms (Continued)

Capital Sins
Cardinal(s) (only when used with
    proper names)
Cardinal Virtues
Chosen People
Christian(s)
Church
College of Bishops
Commandment (one of the Ten or
    Two Great)
Communion (Holy)
Communion of Saints
Council (Second Vatican only)
Council Fathers (Second
    Vatican only)
Crucifixion (of Christ)
Death (of Christ)
Decalogue
Deposit of Faith
Divine Inspiration
Divine Revelation
Divine Truth
Doctors (of the Church)
Ecumenical Council
Emmanuel
Evangelist(s) (the four)
Fathers (of the Church or Council)
Gospel
Holy City (of Jerusalem)
Holy See
Incarnation
Inspiration
Jewish People
Judgment Day
Kingdom of God
Kingdom of Heaven

Last Day
Last Judgment
Latin Rite
Law (Old Testament Law)
Liturgy of the Hours
Lord's Day
Magisterium
Mystical Body of Christ
New Testament
Old Testament
Original Sin
Paschal (Mystery, Sacrifice)
Passion (in reference to
    Christ's Passion)
Pentateuch
People of God
Pope (as specific designation, e.g.,
    Pope Benedict XVI)
Prophets, the Law and the
Purgatory
Reign of God
Resurrection (of Christ)
Revelation
Roman Pontiff
Sabbath (as day of the week)
Satan
Scripture(s) (Sacred, Holy)
Second Vatican Council
Temple, Jerusalem
Ten Commandments
Tradition (Sacred)
Trinity, Holy
Trinitarian
Twelve, the
Word (referring to Jesus)
Word of God (referring to Bible)

Lowercased

angels
apostles (apart from the Twelve)
apostolic
biblical
bishop(s) (when not used with or in place of name)
brother(s)
canon of Scripture
canon law (unless part of title of book)
cardinal(s) (when not used with or in place of name)
Catholic social teaching
church (adj. or as building)
commandment (unless part of proper name)
conciliar (adj.)
confession
cross (not Christ's)
deacon(s) (when not used with or in place of name)
demons
episcopate, episcopacy
father(s) (when not used with or in place of name)
gospel (adj.)
heaven

hell
hierarchy
holy water
marriage
mystery
original justice
pope (when not used with or in place of name)
precepts of the Church
priest(s)
prophet (generic)
psalm(s) (if not the Book of Psalms)
redemption
resurrection (of the dead)
rite (when not used with the name)
rosary (the object)
sabbath (as modifier)
sacrament(s) (when not used with the name)
sacramental(s)
sacrifice of Christ
scriptural
second coming
sister(s)
social teaching (Catholic)
synoptic
tabernacle

ABBREVIATIONS

Acronyms and abbreviations

Spell out all names upon first reference. Then note the desired acronym or abbreviation in parentheses. The acronym/abbreviation may be used thereafter.

Example: The Catholic Campaign for Human Development (CCHD) will issue its annual report next month. CCHD programs are funded through an annual collection in parishes each year.

Initials

For names abbreviated by initials, separate the initials with spaces:

Incorrect: E.B. White

Correct: E. B. White

An exception is the United States, which is abbreviated "U.S." only as an adjective.

Bible

Citations

For citations listing chapters and verses, use these forms: Mt 3:10, 17-18; Jn 10:12, 14:3. Place the citation after the quote but before the period when the citation appears within a paragraph of text. For block quotes, which are separate from the rest of text, place the citation after the period.

Example: "Love one another" (Jn 13:34).

The following citation abbreviations are frequently used in biblical citations:

f.	and following verse
ff.	and following verses

cf.	confer, compare, contrast with
see	for additional information

Abbreviating books

When referencing a book of the Bible in text, give the name in full. Abbreviate books of the Bible in notes and citations. Do not italicize either the book or the abbreviation. Note that no period is used in Bible abbreviations.

OLD TESTAMENT

Genesis	Gn	Proverbs	Prv
Exodus	Ex	Ecclesiastes	Eccl
Leviticus	Lv	Song of Songs	Sg (Song)
Numbers	Nm	Wisdom	Wis
Deuteronomy	Dt	Sirach	Sir
Joshua	Jos	Isaiah	Is
Judges	Jgs	Jeremiah	Jer
Ruth	Ru	Lamentations	Lam
1 Samuel	1 Sm	Baruch	Bar
2 Samuel	2 Sm	Ezekiel	Ez
1 Kings	1 Kgs	Daniel	Dn
2 Kings	2 Kgs	Hosea	Hos
1 Chronicles	1 Chr	Joel	Jl
2 Chronicles	2 Chr	Amos	Am
Ezra	Ezr	Obadiah	Ob
Nehemiah	Neh	Jonah	Jon
Tobit	Tb	Micah	Mi
Judith	Jdt	Nahum	Na
Esther	Est	Habakkuk	Hb
1 Maccabees	1 Mc	Zephaniah	Zep
2 Maccabees	2 Mc	Haggai	Hg
Job	Jb	Zechariah	Zec
Psalms	Ps	Malachi	Mal

NEW TESTAMENT

Matthew	Mt	1 Timothy	1 Tm
Mark	Mk	2 Timothy	2 Tm
Luke	Lk	Titus	Ti
John	Jn	Philemon	Phlm
Acts of the Apostles	Acts	Hebrews	Heb
Romans	Rom	James	Jas
1 Corinthians	1 Cor	1 Peter	1 Pt
2 Corinthians	2 Cor	2 Peter	2 Pt
Galatians	Gal	1 John	1 Jn
Ephesians	Eph	2 John	2 Jn
Philippians	Phil	3 John	3 Jn
Colossians	Col	Jude	Jude
1 Thessalonians	1 Thes	Revelation	Rev
2 Thessalonians	2 Thes		

Common Church Sources

Citations

Citations for common sources from the Church's Magisterium may abbreviate the source name using the abbreviations below, provided that either (1) the full name is spelled out upon first reference, with the abbreviation noted in parentheses, or (2) the publication has an abbreviations list.

Do not italicize abbreviations for the titles of common church sources.

Some common abbreviations

Here are abbreviations for the most commonly cited sources.

GENERAL SOURCES

Catechism of the Catholic Church	CCC
Code of Canon Law (Codex Iuris Canonici)	CIC
Code of Canons of the Eastern Churches (Codex Canonum Ecclesiarum Orientalium)	CCEO

SECOND VATICAN COUNCIL: MAJOR DOCUMENTS

Lumen Gentium (Dogmatic Constitution on the Church)	LG
Dei Verbum (Dogmatic Constitution on Divine Revelation)	DV
Sacrosanctum Concilium (Constitution on the Sacred Liturgy)	SC
Gaudium et Spes (Pastoral Constitution on the Church in the Modern World)	GS
Christus Dominus (Decree on the Pastoral Office of Bishops in the Church)	CD
Presbyterorum Ordinis (Decree on the Ministry and Life of Priests)	PO
Ad Gentes Divinitus (Decree on the Church's Missionary Activity)	AG

Other Vatican/ papal sources

In the back of the *Catechism of the Catholic Church* (2nd ed.) is a list of other common abbreviations for Vatican and papal sources, as well as Vatican congregations. Do not italicize the abbreviations.

In general, abbreviate Vatican and papal sources using the initials of the Latin title (*incipit*): e.g., Pope John Paul II's *Pastores Dabo Vobis* (*I Will Give You Shepherds*) would be abbreviated PDV.

| *USCCB sources* | USCCB sources are less commonly abbreviated. |

Religious Orders

| *General rule* | Do not use periods in abbreviations for religious orders (e.g., SJ, SSND). |
| *CNS Stylebook* | For a complete list of abbreviations for religious orders, see appendices of the *CNS Stylebook on Religion*. |

Degrees

| *Periods* | Do not use periods in abbreviations for either ecclesiastical or academic degrees. |
| *Spelled out* | When spelling out the names of degrees, spell out the formal name ("master of arts," "bachelor of science"). Use apostrophes for less formal references ("master's degree," "bachelor's degree"—but "doctorate"). Note that none of these are capitalized. |

States

| *In text* | In text for publication, always spell out the name of the state. For fund-raising campaigns/collections, it is acceptable to use the zip abbreviations given below. |
| *In citations* | In notes and citations, use postal, or zip, abbreviations for states. |

Alabama	AL	Montana	MT
Alaska	AK	Nebraska	NE
Arizona	AZ	Nevada	NV
Arkansas	AR	New Hampshire	NH

California	CA	New Jersey	NJ
Colorado	CO	New Mexico	NM
Connecticut	CT	New York	NY
Delaware	DE	North Carolina	NC
D.C. (see below)	DC	North Dakota	ND
Florida	FL	Ohio	OH
Georgia	GA	Oklahoma	OK
Hawaii	HI	Oregon	OR
Idaho	ID	Pennsylvania	PA
Illinois	IL	Rhode Island	RI
Indiana	IN	South Carolina	SC
Iowa	IA	South Dakota	SD
Kansas	KS	Tennessee	TN
Kentucky	KY	Texas	TX
Louisiana	LA	Utah	UT
Maine	ME	Vermont	VT
Maryland	MD	Virginia	VA
Massachusetts	MA	Washington	WA
Michigan	MI	West Virginia	WV
Minnesota	MN	Wisconsin	WI
Mississippi	MS	Wyoming	WY
Missouri	MO		

District of Columbia   For the District of Columbia, provide the full name when it is mentioned without "Washington." When paired with Washington, it is abbreviated "D.C." in text, and "DC" in citations. Note that because the District of Columbia is not a state, it is not included in state counts and is typically mentioned separately.

Example: The bishops visited nine states and the District of Columbia.

Example: The tourists flock to Washington, D.C., in the spring.

Example: [1]   USCCB, *United States Catholic Catechism for Adults* (Washington, DC: USCCB, 2006).

Do not use periods to abbreviate the four quadrants of the District of Columbia (NE, NW, SE, SW).

Example: United States Conference of
Catholic Bishops
3211 Fourth Street, NE
Washington, DC 20017

CHAPTER 5
Names and Titles of People and Things

CHURCH ROLES: USE OF TITLES

Saints

Use "St." when preceding the name. Use "saint" when no name follows.

Popes

When using "His Holiness" or "Holy Father," ensure that the identity of the pope in question is clear.

Cardinals

"Cardinal" precedes the name in U.S. usage: "Cardinal Joseph Bernardin," not "Joseph Cardinal Bernardin." Only use "His/Your Eminence" in direct quotes or in the salutation of a letter.

Bishops

Use "Most Rev." or "Most Reverend" before the name for the most formal use (e.g., correspondence). Use "Bishop" or "Archbishop" before the name otherwise. Only use "His/Your Excellency" in direct quotes or in a letter salutation.

Monsignors

Abbreviate as "Msgr." "The Rev. Msgr." is reserved for the most formal occasions. Spell out and capitalize "Monsignor" if referring to the person without the name.

Priests

Abbreviate as "Fr." preceding the name; spell out and capitalize "Father" if referring to the person without the name. It is also sometimes acceptable to use no title before the name if the religious order follows the name (e.g., "John Smith, SJ"). Use "the Rev." only for formal use. In formal writing, use the last name, not first, with the title: e.g., "Fr. Doe," not "Fr. John."

Deacons	Use "Deacon," not "Rev. Mr." (e.g., "Deacon John Smith").
Sisters	Abbreviate as "Sr." before the name. Spell out and capitalize "Sister" if referring to the person without her name. In formal writing, use the last name, not first, with the title: e.g., "Sr. Doe," not "Sr. Jane."
Brothers	Abbreviate "Br." before the name. Spell out and capitalize "Brother" if referring to the person without his name. In formal writing, use the last name, not first, with the title: e.g., "Br. Doe," not "Br. John."
Others	Do not abbreviate "Abbot," "Abbess," or "Mother."

OTHER FORMS OF ADDRESS

A comprehensive guide to forms of public address for civil, military, and professional titles may be found in Chapter 8 of the *Chicago Manual of Style* (15th edition).

PRAYERS AND SACRED TEXTS

Traditional prayers	Treat the names of traditional prayers as proper nouns, not as titles of creative works:

Our Father, Hail Mary, Prayer of St. Francis, the *Memorare*

Note in the example that names in other languages are italicized because they include foreign words.

Newly composed prayers

Prayers that are more recent original works are identified with quotation marks, like any other title of a short work: e.g., "Litany of the Way," "Prayer for Healing."

Scriptures and other principal texts

Like the Bible, the principal texts of other religions are typically treated as proper nouns, not as the titles of works.

Bible, Torah, Talmud, Qur'an, Hadith, Bhagavad Gita

Further, the correct names for the parts of the Catholic Bible are "Old Testament" and "New Testament." Do not use "Hebrew Scriptures" or "Christian Scriptures."

LATIN TITLES (OR *INCIPITS*)

Incipits

Latin "titles" are not technically titles at all—they are actually the first two to three words, or "*incipit*," of the Vatican or papal text in Latin. Thus, the capitalization of Latin "titles" requires careful consideration of audience and purpose. See below.

Capitalization

In a publication for a general audience, capitalize Latin titles as you would capitalize titles in English. That is, capitalize all words except prepositions and articles.

Example: [1]   See John Paul II, *That They All May Be One* (*Ut Unum Sint*), nos. 89-90.

In a publication for a more scholarly church audience, give the Latin *incipit* in sentence-case: that is, capitalize only the first word and subsequent proper nouns, and otherwise lowercase.

Examples: [1]   See John Paul II, *That They All May Be One* (*Ut unum sint*), nos. 89-90.
[2]   See Second Vatican Council, *Decree on the Pastoral Office of Bishops in the Church* (*Christus Dominus*), no. 14. *["Dominus" is a proper noun.]*

Placement with English titles

In a publication aimed at a general audience, provide the English title first, followed by the Latin in parentheses.

When the publication is aimed at an audience more familiar with the Latin titles, give the Latin titles first, followed by the English in parentheses.

Abbreviations

Whether the English or the Latin title is given priority (see above), always use the abbreviation corresponding to the Latin title. (E.g., the *Constitution on the Sacred Liturgy* [*Sacrosanctum Concilium*] is abbreviated SC.) See the "Abbreviations" section of Chapter 4 for a list of abbreviations for common church sources; see also the *Catechism of the Catholic Church*'s Abbreviations section for a fuller list.

USCCB NAME HISTORY

Name changes

The USCCB has undergone several name changes since 1917:

1917-1919	National Catholic War Council
1919-1922	National Catholic Welfare Council
1922-1966	National Catholic Welfare Conference

1966-2001	National Conference of Catholic Bishops (ecclesiastical body); United States Catholic Conference (legal body)
2001-present	United States Conference of Catholic Bishops

Do not use "U.S. Conference of Catholic Bishops," as this is not the legal name of the USCCB.

Updating reprints

Typically, in reprints, only the cover, title page, copyright page, and any contact information are updated to reflect the current name of the Conference. These change to reflect our continuing copyright; other mentions throughout the reprint do not change, in order to maintain the historical integrity of the document.

Citing older works

When referring to older works in new manuscripts, cite the United States Conference of Catholic Bishops as publisher (and as author, where applicable). This practice reflects our continuing copyright of the material.

CHAPTER 6

The Internet

REFERRING TO THE INTERNET

Internet lingo

The following are the preferred capitalization and spelling for common Internet terms:

electronic mailing list	online
e-mail	URL, URLs
Internet	Web site
list service	Web page
	webmaster

Do not use the term "listserv" (or "listserve") to describe an electronic mailing list, because the term is a trademarked brand name. "List service" or "e-mail list" is acceptable.

Internet addresses

Always italicize URLs and e-mail addresses. Do not put them in quotation marks; do not use boldface or underlining. (Automatic underlining in MS Word can be turned off.)

Omit "http://" and other such "protocol" or "channel" tags from URLs. (Web servers, which handle all such URLs, can determine what protocol or channel to use when a URL is typed in.)

Incorrect: For more information, visit http://www. usccb.org/news.

Correct: For more information, visit *www.usccb. org/news.*

Correct: [1] USCCB Office of Child and Youth
Protection, "Who We Are," *United
States Conference of Catholic Bishops,
www.usccb.org/ocyp/whoweare.htm*
(accessed December 16, 2004).

Citing online sources See "Special Cases: Online Sources" in the documentation and citation section of Chapter 3, "Other People's
Words," for guidelines about citing online sources.

COPYRIGHTS/PERMISSIONS ON THE INTERNET

Using Material from Other Sites

Public domain? Material posted on a Web site, even if the page does
not have a copyright notice, is not necessarily in the
public domain. Seek permission to use this material, as
with any other published material.

*Obtaining
permission* Typically, a Web site's owner posts contact
information on the site. In seeking permission, it is
especially important to confirm the ownership of the
material, as many Web sites draw materials from a
variety of sources that may not be credited.

Seeking Permission to Post Copyrighted Material onto
the USCCB Site

Digital rights In order to post onto the USCCB Web site any material (text, photos, artwork, etc.) copyrighted by others,
digital rights must be obtained. Not all copyright own-
ers are willing to grant such rights; and, in some cases,
an additional charge may be levied. If digital rights
cannot be obtained and the use exceeds the limits of
fair use, the material may not be posted.

Downloading	If posted material is intended for downloading and distribution (for example, a bulletin insert), sublicensing rights are needed for all copyrighted materials that exceed fair use. Since these rights may be difficult to obtain, avoid using material copyrighted by others on such projects, if at all possible. For example, using photographs on a bulletin insert may mean that parishes cannot download it for distribution.
Releases	Because of the reach of the Internet, take extra care to obtain any necessary permissions and/or releases. See the end of Chapter 3, "Other People's Words," for a section on releases.

PUBLISHING TO THE INTERNET

Why Publish to the Internet

Internet is *publishing*	Posting a text on the Internet *is* "publishing." While the technology, availability, and reader experience of Internet publications are different from those of printed publications, the fundamental purpose of "publishing" remains unchanged: to disseminate, to make public.
Affordable alternative	Publishing to the Internet—as HTML text, a downloadable PDF file, or an adaptable text file—is an affordable, viable alternative to producing, warehousing, and fulfilling orders for a printed product.

Policies

Posting	Policies governing what material may be posted to the USCCB Web site, and what processes to follow for the different types of postings, are described in the "USCCB Internet Guidelines." Obtain a copy from the staff-only

Web site, *staff.usccb.org*. Consult IT, the Digital Media office, or the General Secretariat for further guidance.

Linking

Links to other Web sites (external to USCCB) require approval from your department director and the General Secretariat. Obtain the form entitled "Conference Web Link Approval Form" from the staff-only Web site, *staff.usccb.org*. Consult IT or the General Secretariat for further guidance.

End User Considerations

Formats

HTML

Posting your publication in HTML format—meaning that the text will appear on a Web page—is ideal when you want to deliver plain text for onscreen reading, when you can allow time for the Digital Media office to convert the text to HTML, and when you want the text to download to readers' computers most quickly. Consult Digital Media for the best way to submit files for the conversion process (including, but not limited to, how to handle citations, graphics, and sidebars). For very long documents, consider working with Digital Media to develop an "index page," a table of contents with links to the chapters or other parts of the document for ease of navigation.

PDF

Posting a PDF to the Conference Web site is desirable when you want to deliver a document in a specific format or design, when time is short (PDFs can be created and posted in minutes), or when you want the document to be easily printed and replicated by the end user (such as bulletin inserts). The product will not be read as a Web page but will instead be a file that the end user can download, save on the computer, and read and print in Acrobat Reader (free) or other PDF viewing software. Consult Digital Media or Publishing about considerations of size, length, and other formatting needs.

Word/RTF file   For documents that should be adaptable by the end user (such as lesson plans or sample letters), consider posting the file as a Word or RTF ("rich text format") document.

CHAPTER 7
Prefatory Statements, Decrees, and Copyright Notices

PREFATORY STATEMENTS

All USCCB resources published for the public must feature a prefatory statement from the General Secretary indicating level of authority. (The following do not require prefatory statements: press releases, action alerts, statements of the Conference president and committee chairs.)

Committee resource

For documents that are developed as a resource of a particular committee:

The document **[title]** was developed as a resource by the **[committee name]** of the United States Conference of Catholic Bishops (USCCB). It was reviewed by the committee chairman, **[Arch]**bishop **[Name]**, and has been authorized for publication by the undersigned.

[General Secretary's full name]
General Secretary, USCCB

Administrative Committee

For documents that receive approval of the Administrative Committee to be published in its own name:

The document **[title]** was developed by the **[committee name]** of the United States Conference of Catholic Bishops (USCCB). It was approved by the Administrative Committee of the USCCB at its **[March/September]** **[year]** meeting for publication in the name of the

Administrative Committee and has been authorized for publication by the undersigned.

[General Secretary's full name]
General Secretary, USCCB

Administrative Committee and developing committee

For a document that receives approval of the Administrative Committee to be published in the name of the committee that developed it:

The document **[title]** was developed by the **[committee name]** of the United States Conference of Catholic Bishops (USCCB). It was approved by the Administrative Committee of the USCCB at its **[March/September] [year]** meeting as a document of the **[committee name]** and has been authorized for publication by the undersigned.

[General Secretary's full name]
General Secretary, USCCB

USCCB full body

For documents that receive approval by the full body:

The document **[title]** was developed by the **[committee name]** of the United States Conference of Catholic Bishops (USCCB). It was approved by the full body of the USCCB at its **[June/November] [year]** General Meeting and has been authorized for publication by the undersigned.

[General Secretary's full name]
General Secretary, USCCB

USCCB and Holy See

For USCCB documents that receive approval by the full body and also receive the *recognitio* of the Holy See:

The document **[title]** was developed by the **[committee name]** of the United States Conference of Catholic Bishops (USCCB). It was approved by the full body of the USCCB at its **[June/November] [year]** General Meeting, received the subsequent *recognitio* of the Holy See, and has been authorized for publication by the undersigned.

[General Secretary's full name]
General Secretary, USCCB

See the next section on publishing the Vatican decrees for these kinds of documents.

DECREES

For a document approved by the USCCB that is subsequently approved by the Holy See, include the full text of all accompanying decrees at the beginning of the publication, including the Vatican protocol number of each decree.

COPYRIGHT NOTICES

SECTION B
NUTS AND BOLTS

CHAPTER 8
Words

SENSITIVITY IN LANGUAGE

American or U.S.

"U.S." preferred

Since "American" may refer to the continents of North or South America, "U.S." is preferred as the adjective pertaining to the United States of America.

"American Church" or "U.S. Church"

Do not use either "American Church" or "U.S. Church" as a synonym for the Church in the United States. Acceptable forms are "Church in the United States," "Church (or Catholic Church) in North America," "Church in South America," or "Church in the Americas." "Catholics in the United States" can also be used.

"U.S. bishops"

Do not refer to the USCCB as "U.S. bishops" or "U.S. Catholic bishops." Acceptable references are "Catholic bishops of the United States" or "bishops of the United States."

USCCB name

Do not use "U.S. Conference of Catholic Bishops." The legal name of the organization is "United States Conference of Catholic Bishops."

Race

Capitalization	Terms of race, ethnicity, or religion that derive from a proper noun are usually capitalized (e.g., "Hispanic/ Latino," "Christian"). Following *Chicago Manual of Style*, section 8.43, "designations based loosely on color are usually lowercased, though capitalization may be appropriate if the writer strongly prefers it."
No hyphens	Do not hyphenate African American, Asian American, Native American, and so forth.
African American, africentric	Take care to distinguish between "African Americans" and other people of African descent (both in the Americas and around the world). Note, however, that "African American" can be used to denote people of African descent living in Central and South America.

Use "africentric," not "afrocentric," when describing something centering on Africa. |
| *When in doubt* | For additional guidance on the use of racial, ethnic, or religious terms, consult the USCCB Offices for Cultural Diversity and for Ecumenical and Interreligious Affairs. |

Gender

Inclusive language	Avoid using "he" when referring to people in general, both men and women. Instead, either use "he or she" (not "s/he") in the singular, or change all references to plural and use "they." (In written communication, "they" is not an acceptable gender-neutral singular pronoun.)

Incorrect:	An individual must account for his actions.
Incorrect:	An individual must account for their actions.

Correct:	All must account for their actions.
Correct:	Each person must account for his or her actions.

Non-gendered nouns   Use words such as "layperson" instead of "layman," and "altar server" instead of "altar boy." "Chairman" is appropriate for the chair of bishops' committees; in all other cases, "chair" or "chairperson" is preferred.

Church: She or it?   The normal usage in liturgical, doctrinal, and catechetical materials is the feminine pronoun. In other kinds of materials (e.g., legal documents), the neuter pronoun may be more appropriate.

God and Trinity   All persons of the Trinity are referred to with masculine pronouns.

Disabilities and Disadvantages

Emphasize person   Place the person before the disability or disadvantage.

INSTEAD OF . . .	USE . . .
Blind person	Person who is blind
Autistic child	Child with autism
Handicapped	Person/people with disabilities
Shut-ins	Those confined to home
At-risk youth	Youth in high-risk environments

Community terms   Some people with disabilities or disadvantages identify themselves as members of distinct communities and cultures. Be cautious about using such terms, and check with Publishing or community resources when in doubt. This kind of language evolves continually, so it is important to stay current with the sensibilities of the communities in question. For example, a "person who is deaf" is someone who has a hearing disability. But a "Deaf" person refers specifically to the community of people with hearing disabilities who identify with Deaf culture, which includes various sign languages, distinct art forms and customs, and common understandings.

COMMON WORD DIFFICULTIES

Misused Words

Comprise

"Comprise" is often confused with "compose." "Is comprised of" is incorrect; the correct usage is "comprises" or "is composed of." The whole comprises the parts, and the parts compose the whole.

Incorrect: The legislative branch is comprised of the House and the Senate.

Correct: The legislative branch is composed of the House and the Senate.

Correct: The legislative branch comprises the House and the Senate.

Correct: The House and Senate compose the legislative branch.

That, which

"That" is used to provide necessary identifying information, with no comma. "Which" is used only when what follows is not necessary to identify what is being described, and it is set off with a comma.

Incorrect: The parish which is on Division Street is undergoing renovations.

Correct: The parish that is on Division Street is undergoing renovations. *["That is on Division Street" is needed to identify what parish is discussed.]*

Correct:	The parish, which is on Division Street, is undergoing renovations. *[Sentence simply notes, as an aside, that the parish in question is on Division Street.]*

Affect, effect

When referring to the impact something has on something else, "effect" is a noun; "affect" is a verb.

Effect (n.):	September 11 had a tremendous *effect* on the nation.
Affect (v.):	September 11 *affected* the nation tremendously.

When "effect" is used as a verb, it means "to accomplish" or "to bring about."

Effect (v.):	The European Union has *effected* great changes in how European countries view themselves. *[I.e., "brought about," not "had an impact on."]*

Likewise, "affect" can also be a noun, referring to one's ability to feel emotion.

Affect (n.):	The student manifested a distinct lack of *affect*, illustrated by her sullenness and lack of response to the sad story.

Ensure, insure, assure

Because these words have similar sounds and meanings, they are often used interchangeably. However, their nuances should be observed when using them:

Ensure:	We must *ensure* that such thefts never happen again. *["Ensure" means "make sure."]*
Assure:	We must *assure* the staff that steps are being taken to prevent future break-ins. *["Assure" means "reassure."]*

Insure:	We must *insure* our property against future losses. *["Insure" refers specifically and only to insurance.]*

U.S., United States   "United States" is the noun. Use "U.S." only as an adjective.

Example:	The U.S. Congress is considering raising the retirement age.
Example:	The bishops of the United States issued a new pastoral plan.

E.g. vs. i.e.   These are commonly confused and erroneously used interchangeably. Knowing what they abbreviate clarifies their usage:

	LATIN	ENGLISH USAGE
e.g.	*exempli gratia*	for example
i.e.	*id est*	that is (usually with a comma)

Note that both are followed by a comma: e.g., like this.

AD vs. BC   The Church typically marks time from the birth of Christ—"AD" (*anno domini,* "the year of our Lord") and "BC" ("before Christ"). AD grammatically precedes the year, while BC comes after the year. (For example, "AD 381" means "the year of our Lord 381.")

Even though "CE" ("Common Era") and "BCE" ("Before the Common Era") are also in use instead of AD and BC, respectively, the USCCB preference is not to use them.

Letters of the Alphabet

Letters as letters   Individual letters and combinations, when referred to as letters, are italicized to make clear that they are intentional.

the letter *m*, a capital *Q*

Plurals of letters   Letters, when referred to as letters, are pluralized with an apostrophe-*s*. (This is a rare exception to the general rule not to use apostrophes to pluralize.)

Example: Sign your name by the two *X*'s.

Working with Words

Words as words   Put words in quotation marks when they are used as words. Do not italicize for this purpose. Also, only combine quotation marks with italics if the word is also foreign (see next item).

Example: I don't know what you mean by the word "inferior."

Do not use single quotation marks for this purpose.

Foreign words   Words foreign to the document's language are put in italic type (except for common abbreviations like "e.g." and "ibid."). When a foreign word is treated as a word, the word—which is already italicized—is put into quotation marks.

Example: I don't know what you mean by *"de iure."*

Brand names and trademarks   Brand names that are trademarked should be capitalized. Whenever possible, use the general term for something, not the trademarked term. (For example: "worship aid" instead of "Missalette®," "electronic mailing list" instead of "LISTSERV®," "photocopy" instead of "Xerox®.")

HYPHENATION

General guide

See *Chicago Manual of Style* (15th ed.), section 7.90, for excellent general guidelines on hyphenating words.

Adjective with noun

Hyphenate an adjective-noun compound when it precedes and modifies another noun.

middle-class values

well-known bishop

Do not hyphenate such a phrase when it follows a verb, making each part function separately.

The bishop was well known.

Common base word

When two or more hyphenated compounds have a common base, omit the base in all but the last. In unhyphenated compounds written as one word, the base can be repeated.

sixth-, seventh-, and eighth-graders
presurgical and postsurgical
himself or herself; him- or herself

Compound adjective

Hyphenate a compound adjective when it precedes what it describes.

step-by-step instructions

up-to-date schedule

However, when the adjective follows the noun it describes, it is not hyphenated.

The schedule was up to date.

Fractions	Hyphenate fractions used as adjectives. Do not hyphenate fractions used as nouns.

Example: A two-thirds majority was needed.

Example: Two thirds of the donations go back to the community.

Adverb plus adjective	Do not put a hyphen after any word ending in "-ly." Hyphens are optional after other adverbs; if ambiguity is possible, a hyphen is warranted.

Poorly attired man

Highly developed system

Less-appreciated art *[hyphen optional]*

Ever-more-resentful neighbor *[hyphens optional]*

Awkward letter constructions	On occasion, a hyphen is used after a prefix or before a suffix to avoid an awkward combination of letters or a potentially misunderstood word (e.g., "bell-like," "re-creation" ["creating again" versus "recreation"]). See dictionary for correct spelling.

Prefixes	Generally, do not hyphenate most words formed with prefixes. Prefixes are usually connected to the base word, as with "hypersensitive," "antiwar," "infrastructure."

anti	intra	re
co	macro	semi
de	micro	sub
hyper	supra	non
hypo	trans	post
infra	un	pre

En-dash (N-dash)   Use en-dashes (–) to form a compound word (instead of a hyphen) when one part of the compound itself consists of two words or a hyphenated word (e.g., Baltimore–New York train; Libreria Editrice Vaticana–United States Conference of Catholic Bishops publication). See Chapter 9, "Grammar and Punctuation Notes," for other discussion of the en-dash.

PREFERRED SPELLINGS

The following list gives preferences for some words that can be spelled or hyphenated in a variety of ways.

(arch)diocese *(not "arch/diocese")*	flier	onsite
co-worker	follow-up	part-time
decision making, decision maker (n.)	full-time (adj./adv.)	policy making, policy maker (n.)
decision-making (adj.)	fund raising, fund raiser (n.)	policy-making (adj.)
diocese-wide *(not "diocesan-wide")*	fund-raising (adj.)	stand-alone
e-mail	interreligious	timeline
fieldwork	Jesus' (irregular poss.)	webmaster
firsthand (secondhand, etc.)	laypeople, layperson	Web site, Web page
	lifelong	worshiping, worshiper
	long-term	
	low-income	
	ongoing	
	online	

CHAPTER 9
Grammar and Punctuation Notes

This chapter does not detail all rules of punctuation and grammar. Rather, it provides notes on common errors and other principles that differ between various styles.

GRAMMAR NOTES

Bulleted and Numbered Lists

Run-in lists

When a numbered or lettered list runs sequentially in the paragraph itself (that is, not itemized vertically), surround each number or letter with parentheses. Do not use periods or a single parenthesis.

Incorrect: Her parish experience is broad and includes 1) running the parish Web site, 2) serving as council president for two terms, and 3) helping with ministry of hospitality.

Incorrect: Her parish experience is broad and includes 1. running the parish Web site, 2. serving as council president for two terms, and 3. helping with ministry of hospitality.

Correct: Her parish experience is broad and includes (1) running the parish Web site, (2) serving as council president for two terms, and (3) helping with ministry of hospitality.

Colons

If the list is introduced by a complete sentence, a colon can be used. If the introducing sentence is incomplete, then do not use a colon.

Incorrect: Her parish experience is broad and includes:
- Running the parish Web site
- Serving as council president for two terms
- Helping with ministry of hospitality

Correct: Her parish experience is broad and includes
- Running the parish Web site
- Serving as council president for two terms
- Helping with ministry of hospitality

Correct: Her parish experience is broad and includes the following:
- Running the parish Web site
- Serving as council president for two terms
- Helping with ministry of hospitality

How to Format Bulleted or Numbered Vertical Lists

Capitalizing

Capitalize the first word of each item.

Hanging indents

Do not insert a hard return after each line and tab over subsequent lines. Instead, set a hanging indent in the word processing software.

Punctuating

If each item is a complete sentence, end it with a period. (If one item is a complete sentence, all should be complete sentences.) See example.

Example: Her parish experience is broad:
- She ran the parish Web site.
- She served as council president for two terms.
- She helped with the ministry of hospitality as an usher.

If the items in the list are not complete sentences, do not punctuate as if they were in a series—the act of bulleting or numbering makes this punctuation redundant.

Incorrect: Her parish experience is broad and includes
- Running the parish Web site,
- Serving as council president for two terms, and
- Helping with ministry of hospitality.

Incorrect: Her parish experience is broad and includes
- Running the parish Web site;
- Serving as council president for two terms;
- Helping with ministry of hospitality.

Correct: Her parish experience is broad and includes
- Running the parish Web site
- Serving as council president for two terms

Numbers/letters When the vertical list is numbered or lettered, the number or letter should be followed by a period. Do not use parentheses on either side of the letter.

Incorrect: Her parish experience is broad and includes
1) Running the parish Web site;
2) Serving as council president for two terms;
3) Helping with ministry of hospitality.

Incorrect: Her parish experience is broad and includes
(1) Running the parish Web site;
(2) Serving as council president for two terms;
(3) Helping with ministry of hospitality.

Correct: Her parish experience is broad and includes
1. Running the parish Web site
2. Serving as council president for two terms
3. Helping with ministry of hospitality

Active and Passive Voice

Definitions

"Active voice" and "passive voice" refer to the way that verbs relate to subjects in sentences.

In *active voice*, the subject performs the action described by the verb.

Active: The bishop ordained the priest.

In *passive voice*, the subject is acted upon—is actually the "object" or target of the verb. (The one doing the action often appears in the agency phrase "by X" or sometimes not at all.)

Passive: The priest was ordained.

Passive: The priest was ordained by the bishop.

Use of active voice

In general, strive for active voice, because it flows more quickly and reads more directly. Passive voice can make for convoluted and tedious reading when it is used unnecessarily or excessively.

Effective use of passive voice

Use passive voice under certain circumstances:

a.   When responsibility is or needs to be obscure

Example: The money was stolen.

Example: The money was stolen by me.

b.   When the action or the thing acted upon is more important than who did the action (as in scientific or statistical writing)

Example: The survey was administered to 2,600 Catholics (by CARA).

Example: Passive voice may sometimes be used.

Parallel Construction

Definition

In a series—of adjectives, nouns, prepositional phrases, even entire sentences—each item must be "parallel" to (or grammatically the same as) the rest.

Incorrect: The bishop was soft-spoken, bilingual, and from Kansas.

Correct: The bishop was soft-spoken and bilingual and came from Kansas.

Vertical lists

In elaborate bulleted or numbered lists, be sure to make each item parallel.

Incorrect: Her parish experience is broad and includes
- Running the parish Web site *[verb]*
- Serving as council president for two terms *[verb]*
- Ministry of hospitality *[noun]*

Correct: Her parish experience is broad and includes
- Running the parish Web site
- Serving as council president for two terms
- Helping with ministry of hospitality

Common Questions

Split infinitives

Splitting an infinitive (e.g., "to boldly go") is now considered a legitimate construction. Sometimes it is even necessary for clarity and direct expression.

Ending sentences with prepositions

The rule against ending a sentence with a preposition has become more of a suggestion through evolution of the language—especially when complex sentence construction makes the "correct" phrasing more convoluted than the "incorrect" phrasing.

Contractions   While contractions do lend a certain informal quality to writing, their limited use has become acceptable in publications when the aim is an approachable or conversational tone that appeals to a wide audience (e.g., in fund-raising materials).

Conjunctions

To begin sentences   Conjunctions can be used to begin sentences, sparingly, for well-chosen reasons.

To join sentences   Two complete sentences can be joined with a comma and conjunction. Some adverbs are mistakenly used instead of conjunctions, creating run-on sentences.

Conjunctions: and, or, for, nor, but, so, yet

Adverbs: however, therefore, thus, indeed, accordingly, besides, hence

Rather than using a comma with such adverbs to join two complete sentences, use a semicolon.

Incorrect: I won't be able to attend the party, however, I send my best wishes. *[Run-on: "However" is not a conjunction.]*

Correct: I won't be able to attend the party; however, I send my best wishes. *[The semicolon joins two complete sentences without a conjunction.]*

Correct: I won't be able to attend the party, but I send my best wishes.

Plurals

Apostrophes	In general, do not use an apostrophe to form plurals.

Incorrect: The Smith's called to RSVP.

Correct: The Smiths called to RSVP.

One exception is "do's" when part of "do's and don'ts."

Abbreviations, numbers	Do not use apostrophes to pluralize abbreviations or numbers. Simply add an -s in the usual way.

Incorrect: 30's, 1950's, RFP's

Correct: 30s, 1950s, RFPs

Letters	To avoid confusion, use an apostrophe when pluralizing letters (e.g., *x*'s, *y*'s). Note that letters treated as letters are italicized.

PUNCTUATION NOTES

Sentence-Ending Punctuation

Spaces after sentences	Type only one space, not two, after periods, exclamation points, or question marks.

Period

Bulleted list	Omit periods in a vertical list unless one or more of the items are complete sentences. Do not put semicolons or commas after the first items or a period after the final item.

Example: The following dioceses held the collection:
- Chicago
- Los Angeles
- Galveston/Houston

Abbreviations   Use periods after most abbreviations. Exceptions are books of the Bible (Jn or Mt), abbreviations for religious orders (SJ, SSND), and acronyms (IRS, USCCB). Also use periods after initials, with a space between two initials (e.g., A. B. Smith).

Ellipses   Ellipses should be typed as three periods with space between each and a space in front and behind: "he did this . . . and that." Three ellipses points are used in the middle of a sentence. Four are used at the end of a sentence, with no space between the last word and the first period.

Exclamation Point

In general, make sparing use of the exclamation point, reserving it for true exclamations. Avoid using exclamation points to "punch up" or draw attention to key statements—they can actually distract the reader from what is being stated.

Question Mark

Non-questions   Do not put a question mark when a question is indirect or implied, because the sentence is not grammatically a question.

Incorrect:	Our question was whether we should conduct field consultation?
Correct:	Our question was whether we should conduct field consultation.

With quote marks   If the question mark is not part of the quoted phrase, place it outside the quotation marks. If the quoted phrase includes a question, place the question mark inside the quotation marks.

Example: Do you know what it means to be a "community of salt and light"?

Example: He asked, "Do you know what it means to be a 'community of salt and light'?"

Comma

Serial comma   Do use the serial comma (e.g., red, white, and blue).

Compound verb   Do not use a comma to split a compound verb.

Example: The bishop reviewed the first draft of the text and agreed to write the preface. *[No comma between "text" and "and."]*

Compound sentence   Use a comma and a conjunction to join the two independent parts of a compound sentence.

Example: The members voted on two statements, and they raised a number of issues to be discussed at a later meeting.

Jr. and Sr.   Do not use a comma before or after Jr. and Sr.

Example: John F. Kennedy Jr. attended the event.

Dates   Do not use a comma between a month and a year (e.g., April 1995). If the day is added, place commas on both sides of the year.

Example: On July 1, 2000, the National Conference of Catholic Bishops/United States Catholic Conference legally combined and were renamed the United States Conference of Catholic Bishops.

Locations

When identifying a location by city and state, use a comma before and after the state (and/or country, if applicable).

Incorrect: I am going to Dallas, Texas to visit family.

Correct: I am going to Dallas, Texas, to visit family.

Semicolon

Use

Semicolons have only two functions:
1. To join two complete sentences
2. To separate main elements in a complex series where one or more elements include a comma

Joining sentences

A semicolon can be used (instead of a comma and conjunction) to combine two sentences into a compound sentence. Typically, the second sentence is closely related to the first.

Incorrect: I won't be able to attend the party, however, I send my best wishes. *[Join two sentences with a comma and a conjunction. "However" is an adverb, not a conjunction.]*

Correct: I won't be able to attend the party; however, I send my best wishes. *[The semicolon joins two complete sentences without a conjunction.]*

Complex series

The comma is typically used to separate items in a series of three or more things. However, when a single item itself includes commas, then replace the series commas with semicolons to clearly identify the items.

Awkward: The meeting was attended by Publishing, Laity, Marriage, Family Life, and Youth, Migration and Refugee Services, and Catholic Education.

| *Clear:* | The meeting was attended by Publishing; Laity, Marriage, Family Life, and Youth; Migration and Refugee Services; and Catholic Education. |

Colon

Semicolon vs. colon

Use a colon, not a semicolon, to introduce an idea, series, or example.

| *Incorrect:* | USCCB Publishing is offering two new prayer cards; one for Our Lady of Guadalupe and one commemorating the Year of the Eucharist. |

| *Correct:* | USCCB Publishing is offering two new prayer cards: one for Our Lady of Guadalupe and one commemorating the Year of the Eucharist. |

Before lists

Do not use a colon to introduce a list unless what precedes the colon is a complete sentence.

| *Incorrect:* | The professor wanted: a ten-page paper, an annotated bibliography, and a reading-response journal. *["The professor wanted" is not a complete sentence.]* |

| *Correct:* | The professor outlined three course requirements: a ten-page paper, an annotated bibliography, and a reading-response journal. |

Likewise, do not use a colon to introduce a bulleted or numbered list unless it is preceded by a complete sentence.

| *Correct:* | The participating dioceses were
• Chicago
• Los Angeles
• Galveston-Houston |

Parentheses and Brackets

Parentheses

Parentheses set off supplemental or digressive information within the sentence, with minimal intrusion when used sparingly.

Example: The members (despite being used to paper ballots) seemed enthusiastic about the electronic voting machines.

Brackets with parentheses

Brackets are used as subordinated parentheses within parentheses.

Incorrect: The bishops have advocated more intentional outreach to young adults (see *Sons and Daughters of the Light* (1997)).

Correct: The bishops have advocated more intentional outreach to young adults (see *Sons and Daughters of the Light* [1997]).

If there is only one parenthetical expression, use parentheses.

Brackets within quotations

Use brackets within quotes to insert or change quoted material.

Example: "This [guide] complements the encyclical very well."

Dashes

Use

Like parentheses, dashes set off supplemental or digressive information within the sentence. Dashes attract more attention to what they set off than parentheses do.

Example: The members—despite being used to paper ballots—seemed to enthusiastically welcome the electronic voting machines.

Format and spaces	Use the actual dash (—) in word processing documents. Do not use a single hyphen. As an alternative, type two consecutive hyphens (--). In any case, do not put any space before or after a dash.

> *Example:* The members--despite being used to paper ballots--seemed to enthusiastically welcome the electronic voting machines.

Em-dash (M-dash)	"Em-dash" is the technical term for the basic dash (—).

> *Example:* Often we see a lack of solidarity towards our society's weakest members—the old, the sick, immigrants, children—and an indifference toward the world's peoples even when basic values are involved.

En-dash (N-dash)	En-dashes (–) serve two specific and rare purposes in USCCB style:

1. To cite a Scripture passage that spans chapters, not just verses (e.g., Jn 4:3–6:2)
2. To form a compound word (instead of a hyphen) when one part of the compound itself consists of two words or a hyphenated word (e.g., Baltimore–New York train; Libreria Editrice Vaticana–United States Conference of Catholic Bishops publication)

Otherwise, do not use the en-dash. In regular ranges of numbers, use hyphens.

Quotation Marks: Double, Single, and European Style

With punctuation	Place periods and commas inside the quotation marks (assuming no citation follows the quote). If exclamation marks or question marks are part of the quoted material, they also go inside the quotation marks (with a period only after any citation ending the sentence; otherwise it is not needed). Place colons and semicolons outside quotation marks.

Double and single quotation marks

Double quotation marks are primary. Single quotation marks are secondary: use them for quotes within quotes. (Note that British style reverses this usage. When quoting from sources following British style, conform instead to U.S. style. This is an acceptable silent change to quotations.)

Both follow the same punctuation rules. If the two are placed consecutively, do not insert either punctuation or any space between them.

Incorrect:	"Young adults are called to be 'sons and daughters of the light'."
Incorrect:	"Young adults are called to be 'sons and daughters of the light.' "
Correct:	"Young adults are called to be 'sons and daughters of the light.'"

Do not use single quotation marks ('/') for any other uses, including the following: words used as words, emphasis, names of concepts, partial uncited quotes, etc.

Block quotes

Do not use quotation marks around block-indented quotes. Quotations that begin and end within block quotes should use double quotation marks rather than single quotation marks. (See Chapter 3, "Other People's Words," for more discussion of block quotes and other quotation conventions.)

European quotes

Foreign texts and sources, such as Vatican documents, sometimes use European quotation marks («/») instead of U.S. quotation marks ("/"). When quoting from such text, always replace European marks with conventional marks and follow the punctuation rules given above.

Titles within titles	For titles within titles, when both would be italicized individually, retain italics for all and put the internal title in quotation marks.

> *Example:*   *Leader's Guide to "Sharing Catholic Social Teaching"*

Emphasis	Do not use quotation marks for emphasis.

Apostrophe

Plurals	Do not use an apostrophe to form plurals of abbreviations or numbers (e.g., 30s, 1950s, SOSs, RFPs, don'ts). To avoid confusion, the apostrophe is used when pluralizing letters (e.g., *x*'s, *y*'s).
Omitted figures and contractions	Use an apostrophe in place of an omitted figure or letter (e.g., the '30s, don't). Such usage is typically acceptable only in promotional and informal material. Spelling out is preferred (e.g., 1930s, do not).

Hyphen

Spelling	When in doubt, consult the *Chicago Manual of Style* (15th ed.) or a dictionary about correct spelling and hyphenation. (See Chapter 2, "Preferred Editions," for recommended dictionaries.)
	See the hyphenation section of Chapter 8, "Words," for more specific guidelines.
Line breaks	In manuscripts headed for publication, do not hyphenate words in order to break lines. (This will be managed in desktop publishing.)

Hyphens vs. dashes	Do not use a hyphen in place of a regular dash or vice versa, with or without spaces. (See discussion of dashes, above.)

Hyphens should be replaced by en-dashes for only two specific and rare purposes in the house style:

1. To cite a Scripture passage that spans chapters, not just verses (e.g., Jn 4:3–6:2)
2. To form a compound word (instead of a hyphen) when one part of the compound itself consists of two words or a hyphenated word (e.g., Baltimore–New York train; Libreria Editrice Vaticana–United States Conference of Catholic Bishops publication)

Slash

No spaces	Do not surround a slash with spaces in ordinary usage.
Quoting verse	When quoting verse, to avoid actually breaking the lines, use slashes—in this case, with one space on either side—to show where the lines were broken by the original writer. Retain all punctuation.

> *Example:*   Jesus first preached in the synagogue by reading a prophetic passage from Isaiah: "The Spirit of the Lord is upon me, / because he has anointed me / to bring glad tidings to the poor" (Lk 4:18).

CHAPTER 10

Treatment of Numbers

GENERAL GUIDELINES

When to spell out

For publications, spell out numbers (rather than putting numerals) in the following cases:

a. Whole numbers one through one hundred
b. Round numbers ("hundred," "thousand," "million," and so on)
c. Numbers at the beginning of a sentence (e.g., "Two hundred eleven people attended the conference.")
d. Decades ("the sixties"; but "the 1960s")

For campaign/fund-raising materials, spell out only numbers one through nine and provide numerals for ten and above.

When to use numerals

In publications, use numerals in the following cases:

a. Numbers above one hundred
b. Percentages (e.g., 12 percent)
c. Decimals (e.g., 20.5)
d. Dates, addresses, phone numbers
e. Money (e.g., $3 million or $325,254)

For campaign/fundraising materials, spell out only numbers one through nine and provide numerals for ten and above.

Ordinals

Ordinal numbers (e.g., "first," "ninety-ninth," "223rd") follow the same rules as above. Do not superscript the suffixes (if necessary, turn off the auto-correction feature in Microsoft Word).

Percentages   Spell out "percent" in regular usage.

Campaign/fund-raising materials should use the percent symbol.

Over and under   "More than" and "less than" (or "fewer than") are used with quantifiable or countable amounts. "Over" and "under" are used with non-countable amounts (typically percentages or some fractions).

Incorrect:	Over twenty-six apples; more than 6 percent
Correct:	More than twenty-six apples; over 6 percent

Consistency and flexibility   In general, if a group of numbers in a paragraph includes one that should be given in numerals, provide all in numerals.

Example:	Information packets were sent to 33 dioceses, 462 parishes, and 8 seminaries.

If the paragraph includes more than one "category" of numbers—that is, more than one type of thing being enumerated—apply this rule only to the categories meeting this rule, not to the entire paragraph.

Example:	In all, almost 600 tulip bulbs were planted: 215 bulbs in each of the two main flower beds, and more than 150 total in three smaller flower beds.

In this example, the "flower beds" category has no numbers that need to be provided in numerals, so "two" and "three" are spelled out. Two numbers in the "tulip bulbs" category fit the numeral rule, so all numbers of tulips are given in numerals.

SPECIAL NUMBERS

Dates

When the date is just month-year, do not use a comma:

Incorrect:	The bishops approved the statement in November, 2000.
Correct:	The bishops approved the statement in November 2000.

When the date includes the day, use two commas to set off the year:

Incorrect:	On November 15, 2000 the bishops approved the statement.
Correct:	On November 15, 2000, the bishops approved the statement.
Correct:	The bishops approved the statement on November 15, 2000.

Time

Use lowercased "a.m." and "p.m." with periods between. For 12 p.m., use "noon"; for 12 a.m., use "midnight." General time references can be spelled out in the text as well (e.g., "dinner is at seven o'clock"). Use numerals for times that are more specific (e.g., "the 5:40 train").

Units of measure

Measurements follow the same rules as above in nontechnical texts.

Phone numbers

Begin U.S. phone numbers with the area code. Leave off "1-" (but do add international codes when necessary).

CHAPTER 11

Italics, Boldface, and Others

ITALICS

Titles

Italicize proper names of books, journals, works of art, movies, and albums. Do not put these in quotation marks. Exceptions are sacred texts, such as the Bible and the Qur'an, and the names of traditional prayers; in both cases, give the title in plain text. Latin titles are also italicized. Abbreviations of titles are not italicized.

Titles within titles

For titles within titles, when both would be italicized according to the above rule, italicize the full title and put the internal title in quotation marks.

Example: *Leader's Guide to "Sharing Catholic Social Teaching"*

URLs and e-mail addresses

Italicize URLs (Web addresses) and e-mail addresses.

Foreign words

Italicize words in a language other than the document's primary language. (For example, in a Spanish-language document, English words would be italicized.) Do not italicize Latin abbreviations commonly used in citations (e.g., ibid., cf., etc.).

Emphasis

Italics can be used to emphasize a word or phrase, but this should be done sparingly. Try to convey emphasis through the phrasing itself, not through visual weight.

Vs. underlining

In general, use italics and avoid underlining, as the two are technically redundant. (Underlining was originally used in manuscripts to denote italics for typesetting for publication. Word processing software makes italics available to all, so underlining has lost function.)

Quotations	Do not format quotations in italics to identify them as quotations—regardless of whether the quotations appear within the paragraph or are set off as block quotes. (Note that italics appearing in the original quote should be retained, particularly in the case of quotes from papal and Holy See texts.)

BOLDFACING

Emphasis	If a word is to be emphasized, use italics rather than boldfacing. (As mentioned above, try to avoid the need to visually emphasize a word or phrase.)
Headings	As a general rule, boldfaced type is used only to identify higher-priority heading levels.

UNDERLINING

Vs. *italics*	In general, use italics instead of underlining. See above for discussion of italics versus underlining.
URLs *and* e-mail *addresses*	Do not use underlining to denote Internet addresses. (Microsoft Word's automated setting can be turned off to prevent this.)

ALL CAPS AND SMALL CAPS

Bible quotes	The Bible uses small caps to indicate the use of the divine name in the original Hebrew: for example, "Lord" and "I Am" in Exodus. These text styles must

be preserved in quotes from the Bible. Either option, all caps or small caps, is acceptable.

Emphasis   To emphasize a word, use italics rather than all caps.

Headings   Typically, only top-level headings are formatted in all capital letters ("ALL CAPS") or in small capital letters ("SMALL CAPS").

Small caps   The *Chicago Manual of Style* has abandoned small-caps formatting in the traditional places (e.g., A.D. is now AD, P.M. is now p.m.).

APPENDICES

APPENDIX A
Checklist for Preparing Manuscripts for USCCB Publishing

This checklist provides brief guidance for some of the most frequently encountered manuscript preparation needs. Please consult this *USCCB Style Guide* for additional, more detailed information about preparing USCCB documents for publication.

1. File Creation and Formatting

A note concerning the creation of files: please contact Publishing staff to discuss how to set up and/or format an electronic file of a manuscript intended for eventual publication, in order to facilitate accurate and timely production of materials.

2. Quotations and Citations

(See Chapter 3, "Other People's Words," and also Chapter 2, "Preferred Editions.")

- Ensure that quotations match the source word-for-word, and that any changes are clearly marked with ellipses or brackets.
- Cite all quotations, paraphrases, statistics, interviews, and the original ideas of others. When in doubt, cite.
- Use the *New American Bible* as the source for Bible quotations. Use the Flannery or Abbott translations of documents from the Second Vatican Council.

- Cite quotations with complete author, title, publication information, copyright date, etc. Cite the URL, or Web site address, for quotes from online sources.

3. Permissions

(See Chapter 3, "Other People's Words," final section, on copyrights and permissions. When in doubt, consult the Office of General Counsel. See also Chapter 2, "Preferred Editions.")

- Provide photocopies for all quoted and cited material. The photocopies should include the following for each source used: title page, copyright page, and page(s) of quoted or cited material (including statistics).
- Keep copies of all contracts and releases regarding the document, and provide copies to Publishing.
- Quote, where possible, from texts for which permission agreements exist.

4. USCCB Conventions

- When referring to the bishops or the USCCB, replace "U.S. bishops" or "U.S. Catholic bishops" with "Catholic bishops of the United States." Replace "U.S. Conference of Catholic Bishops" with "United States Conference of Catholic Bishops."
- Capitalize important words as indicated in the USCCB Capitalization Guide. (See Chapter 4, "Capitalization and Abbreviation"; see also Chapter 5, "Names and Titles of People and Things").
- Doublecheck abbreviations of books of the Bible. (See Chapter 4, "Capitalization and Abbreviation.")

APPENDIX B
Standard Publication Formats and Length Estimates

This appendix provides length estimates (in words or lines) as guides to writers, editors, and project coordinators when

1. Drafting text of the correct length when the project format is already known
2. Determining the best format for a manuscript already prepared
3. Determining whether a manuscript will fit the format requested

This list is not intended to be exhaustive. It provides common sizes and standard Publishing product formats as guides. Please consult Publishing for guidance on projects not falling easily into these categories.

Definitions

Prayer card   Typically 4x6" card. Two-sided is standard; some are 4-panel 4x6" folded "cards."

Brochure   Typically 4x9". Can run 4, 6, or 8 panels. Can fit in a pamphlet rack or a #10 business envelope. One panel is the cover, and a second typically includes only copyright and marketing information.

Bulletin insert   Typically 8.5x11". Usually runs 2 panels (2-sided, 8.5x11" sheet); can run 4 panels (folded, 11x17" sheet).

Booklet, 4x9"

Generally runs up to 36 published pages in length (including front matter and appendices). Can fit in a pamphlet rack or (if not too thick) a #10 business envelope. Consider switching up to the 6x9" paperback format for texts likely to run longer than 36 pages in 4x9" format.

Paperback, 6x9"

Generally starts at 32 pages in 6x9" layout, with two standard binding options.

Saddlestitched (stapled). Books shorter than 64 pages are best bound using saddlestitching.

Perfect binding (glued, flat spine). Books larger than 64 pages can and should be perfectbound. Books must be 6x9" (trade size), longer than 64 pages, and perfect-bound to qualify for inclusion on the bestseller list of the Catholic Book Publishers Association.

See the following page for a table of length estimates for standard publication formats.

Length Estimates*

FORMAT		LENGTH ESTIMATE
Prayer card (4x6")	1 panel (not includ-ing cover)	*Large type:* 18 lines (est. 7 words per line)
		Small type: 30 lines (est. 8 words per line)
Brochure (4x9")	4 panels	700 words (text-heavy)
	6 panels	1,100 words (text-heavy)
	8 panels	1,500 words (text-heavy)
Bulletin insert (8.5x11")	2 panels	1,700-1,900 words
Booklet (4x9")**	per 4 published pages***	800-1,000 words
Paperback (6x9")**	per 4 published pages***	1,200-1,400 words

* Note that these estimates must include full citations and boilerplate text: copyright notices, prefatory statements, and permission information.

** The guidelines for booklets and paperbacks give word count estimates per 4 published pages of text. After using these estimates to calculate pages of text, remember to add 4-8 pages for front matter, in order to arrive at the estimated page count for an entire book.

*** The page counts of booklets and paperbacks must be divisible by 4 because of how they are printed and bound on press. (For longer paperbacks, a pagination divisible by 8 or 16 is sometimes more cost-effective, again because of how they are manufactured.)

A NOTE ABOUT LANGUAGE EDITIONS

Note that a Spanish translation is typically longer than its English counterpart, by as much as 10%. Estimate Spanish word count accordingly, and then calculate final published length according to the formulae provided in the table above. This guideline is particularly important for bilingual editions.

NOTES

NOTES

NOTES

NOTES

NOTES

NOTES

NOTES